Introduction

Marriage has been defined as the only war where one sleeps with the enemy. Is it a word or a sentence? Mae West said it was an institution, 'but who the hell wants to live in an institution'? John Mortimer said it was like pleading guilty to an indefinite sentence – without parole.

The following pages include various reflections by those who've been burned by the sacrament in one way or another, or maybe in every way possible, as they saw their dreams of bliss to their 'awfully wedded' spouses turning into dust. Some of them have been able to view their experiences with sanguine detachment while others have used a form of gallows humour to deal with their discomfiture. All, in their way, provide cautionary dollops of advice for those of you who may be attempting a leap into something Voltaire called 'the only adventure open to the cowardly.'

Wedding Belles

Wedding Belles

FUNNY QUOTES ABOUT MARRIAGE

COMPILED BY
AUBREY MALONE

YOUCAXTON PUBLICATIONS
OXFORD & SHREWSBURY

YouCaxton Publications
enquiries@youcaxton.co.uk

Contents

Meeting Mr Right

Never ever go to bed with a man on the first date. Not ever.
Unless you really want to. *(Cynthia Heimel)*

I've been on so many blind dates I should get a free dog.
(Wendy Liebman)

I'm still going on bad dates when by now I should be
in a bad marriage. *(Laura Kightlinger)*

The closest I came to a *ménage-a-trios* was when
I dated a schizophrenic. *(Rita Rudner)*

I know nothing about dating. When I started out I was always
trying to avoid saying things like, 'You don't sweat much for
a fat girl.' *(Billy Connolly)*

The only reason I dated my last boyfriend was because I felt too
lazy to commit suicide. *(Judy Tenuta)*

I once had three dates on a single Saturday and still had time to
defrost my refrigerator and rotate my tyres. *(Roz Doyle)*

Whenever I date a guy I think: Is this the man I want my kids to
spend their weekends with? *(Rita Rudner)*

I'm not going on any more dates. If I want to get treated like shit
I'll get married. *(Janeane Garofalo)*

My girlfriend told me she was seeing another man. I told her to
rub her eyes. *(Emo Philips)*

Save a boyfriend for a rainy day and another one
in case it doesn't. *(Mae West)*

I only saw him twice and we have two children.
(Sheilah Graham)

My boyfriend and I broke up. He wanted to get married and I
didn't want him to. *(Rita Rudner)*

I blame myself for my boyfriend's death. I shot him. *(Jo Brand)*

I'm married now so I have to do my dating on the internet.
(Thyra Lees-Smith)

Burt Reynolds once asked me to go out with him. I was in his
room at the time. *(Phyllis Diller)*

I enjoy dating married men because they don't want anything
kinky, like breakfast. *(Joni Rodgers)*

She who hesitates is won. *(Oscar Wilde)*

I refuse to go on blind dates because I have perfect eyesight.
(Ronnie Corbett)

I was dating a transvestite. My mother said, 'Marry him – you'll
double your wardrobe.' *(Joan Rivers)*

I'm in my thirties and I've never really had a boyfriend. The
older I get, the more I realise I'm going to be someone's
second wife. *(Wendy Wilkins)*

My husband chased me until I caught him. *(Pia Zadora)*

She: 'I can't go out with you tonight because
    I'm getting married.'
He: 'Okay, how about tomorrow night?'

If men acted after marriage as they do during courtship
    there would be fewer divorces. And more bankruptcies.
    (Frances Rodman)

I'd love to go out with you but I want to spend more time with
    my blender. *(Rita Rudner)*

While a girl is waiting for the right man to come along, that
    doesn't mean she can't have a wonderful time with all the
    wrong ones. *(Cher)*

It was only after I found Mr. Right that I discovered his middle
    name was Always. *(Marisa Mackle)*

My mother was desperate to get me married. She used to say,
    'Sure he's a murderer. But a *single* murderer.' *(Joan Rivers)*

I'm married to an English guy. He's very reserved. In fact it
    wasn't until a year after we were married that I actually knew
    he wanted to go out with me. *(Kit Hollerbach)*

Quizmaster: 'Name something a girl should know about a man
    before marrying him.'
Contestant: 'His name.'
    (Family Fortunes)

When I look back, my happiest memory is not of the Goons. It's
    of a girl called Julia with enormous breasts. *(Spike Milligan)*

Heading Towards the Altar

I'm getting married on March 28th but I'm not sure
   what year yet. *(Janeane Garofalo)*

I sometimes think that if Adam and Eve were merely engaged
   she would not have talked with the serpent and the world
   would then have been saved an infinity of misery. *(H.G.Wells)*

Did you ever notice that the word 'engaged' has 'gag' in the
   middle of it? *(Rosie O'Donnell)*

The traditional Irish marriage proposal goes like this, 'How
   would you like to be buried with my people?' *(Noel Purcell)*

When I proposed to my husband it wasn't a question.
   It was an order. *(Christine Hamilton)*

My fiancé and I are having a little disagreement. What I want
   is a big church wedding with bridesmaids and flowers and a
   no-expense spared reception. What he wants is to break off
   our engagement. *(Sally Poplin)*

Get dressed. We're going to Tijuana.
   (Ike Turner's marriage proposal to Tina)

I'm not in favour of long engagements. They give people the
   opportunity of finding out each others character before
   marriage – which is never advisable. *(Oscar Wilde)*

It was a dull week in Hollywood when my engagement wasn't
   announced to one man or another. *(Tallulah Bankhead)*

Have you noticed that after women set a date for their
   wedding they invariable become besotted with the size of
   their bottoms? *(Mimi Spencer)*

I've been with the same girl for five years now so I finally
   popped the question: 'Why are we still seeing each other?'
   (Bill Hicks)

The trouble about asking for a woman's hand in marriage
   is the fact that you have to take the rest of her as well.
   (Jimmy O'Dea)

When Woodrow (Wilson) proposed to me I was so surprised I
   nearly fell out of the bed. *(Edith Bolting)*

Before you pop the question you have to question the pop.
   (Jack Cruise)

Will you marry me? Did he leave you any money?
   Answer the second question first.
   (Groucho Marx to a widow in Duck Soup*)*

Before we got engaged he never farted.
   Now it's a second language *(Caroline Rhea)*

Marry me and you'll be farting through silk.
   (Robert Mitchum to his eventual wife Dorothy)

Will you marry me? It's risky, but you'd get fucked regularly.
   (John Osborne's proposal to Penelope Gilliatt. She accepted).

I can honestly say that I always look on Pauline as one of the
   nicest girls I was ever engaged to *(P.G. Wodehouse)*

I asked my girlfriend when she was going to get married but she said, 'Why buy a book when you can join a circulating library? *(Michael Green)*

Few things in life are more embarrassing than having to inform an old friend you've just become engaged to his fiancée. *(W.C. Fields)*

Before accepting a marriage proposal, take a good look at his father. If he's still handsome and has his own teeth, marry him instead. *(Diane Jordan)*

The only question a man asks after 'Will you marry me?' is 'What's for dinner?' *(Gene Perret)*

A marriage proposal is all about timing. And blood-alcohol levels. *(Peter van Dijk)*

I arranged my wedding day for December 29, which meant that the previous six months hard-won weight loss was annihilated in a matter of minutes when I interfaced with a wheelie-bin size box of chocolates. *(Marian Keyes)*

Once a week is quite enough to propose to anyone. *(Oscar Wilde)*

I was engaged to a contortionist but she broke it off. *(Les Dawson)*

Holy Deadlock

The only people who want to get married today are
Catholic priests. *(Mortimer Feinberg)*

Marilyn Monroe married a Protestant, a Catholic and a Jew, in
that order, and divorced all of them impartially, with the
proper amount of tears. That's what I call brotherhood.
(Harry Golden)

My wife converted me to religion. I never believed in hell till I
married her. *(Hal Roach)*

Wedding ceremonies should only be performed at Lourdes
because it obviously takes a miracle to make a marriage work.
(Kathy Lette)

I'm Catholic and my mother said we were born to suffer. So I
married an attorney. *(Maura Lake)*

I'd say Jesus was great crack. Anyone who goes to a wedding
and changes water into a wine has a sense of humour.
(Pat Ingoldsby)

As late as 1954, Pope Pius XII rebuked the subversive views of
those who so exalt marriage as to rank it ahead of virginity.
Whoever believed that should be cast away on a desert island
with at least ten hungry virgins. *(Jack Cardiff)*

It was very good of God to let Carlyle and Mrs. Carlyle marry
one another and so make only two people miserable instead
of four. *(Samuel Butler)*

My husband and I divorced over religious differences. He thought he was God and I didn't. *(Vera Foster)*

My wife is so religious we couldn't get fire insurance for a long time because she had so many candles burning. *(Bob Hope)*

You only have to mumble a few words in church to get married and a few words in your sleep to get divorced. *(Hal Roach)*

You can tell if a priest isn't into mixed marriages. He says things at the service like, 'Isn't it great that these two people from different religions love each other so much that they don't mind going to hell?' *(Judd Apaton)*

Those who marry God can become domesticated too. It's just as humdrum as all the other marriages. *(Graham Greene)*

Great news from the Pope: He's in favour of mixed marriages. One man and one woman. *(Ann Landers)*

In Biblical times a man could have as many wives as he could afford – just like today. *(Abigail van Buren)*

I really think priests should be allowed to marry. If a priest meets another priest and they like one another, what's wrong with them going up the aisle together? *(Dave Allen)*

Christians are only allowed one wife. This is called monotony. *(Sentence in school essay quoted by John G. Muir)*

The main reason for the big security presence at the wedding of Posh Spice and David Beckham was to keep the priests away from the altar boys. *(Patrick Kielty)*

If God didn't mean us to gamble he'd never have invented marriage. *(Noel V. Ginnity)*

I got married at the same age as Christ was when he died. We both suffered. *(James Woods)*

It was a mixed wedding. She was from Glasgow and he was from Edinburgh. *(Stanley Baxter)*

The difference between a Catholic wife and a Jewish one is that a Catholic wife has real orgasms and fake jewellery. *(Jackie Mason)*

Pre-Nups

Since marriage isn't forever any more, real commitment comes
 when you burn the pre-nup. *(Erica Jong)*

The best pre-nup is the one stipulating that you
 never get married. *(Katharine Hepburn)*

I drew up a pre-nuptial arrangement with my wife. If we
 separated, the house was to be split 50-50. She'd get the
 outside and I'd get the inside. *(Pat Redden)*

Any man I was going to marry would be shocked if I didn't ask
 him to sign a pre-nup. *(Madonna)*

Pre-nups are for people who plan to get divorced. *(Jane Graves)*

A pre-nup is when a woman says to her fiancé, 'I'm signing this
 to prove I'm not marrying you for your money even though
 we both know I am.' *(John Crosbie)*

My wife and I have the greatest pre-nup agreement in the world.
 It's called love. *(Gene Perrett)*

The Big Day

The Stag Night should be held sufficiently in advance of the wedding to allow for any prison sentences that might have to be served as a result. *(Jenny Éclair)*

On the morning of the wedding she was in a complete panic. She said, 'I have something old and something new but nothing borrowed or blue.' I said, 'What about your mortgage and your varicose veins?' *(Victoria Wood)*

The trouble between my wife and me started during our marriage service. When I said 'I do', she said, 'Don't use that tone of voice with me'. *(Roy Brown)*

The wedding day is that day of a man's life when he realizes he can't face another date with a legal secretary who wants to be a nightclub comedienne. *(Henny Youngman)*

It was a Scottish wedding – the confetti was elastic. *(Bob Monkhouse)*

It's too bad that in most marriage ceremonies they don't use the word 'obey' anymore. It used to lend a little humour to the occasion. *(Lloyd Cary)*

He noticed that the bride was pregnant so at the wedding everyone threw puffed rice. *(Dick Cavett)*

My husband is the world's greatest procrastinator. When the priest said, 'You may now kiss the bride' he replied, 'Can it not wait till tomorrow?' *(Doris Miller)*

Every bride has to learn it's not her wedding but her mother's.
(Lucy Nugent)

Is it kissomary to cuss the bride? *(Rev. Archibald Spooner)*

Her fantasy of a white wedding came true. It snowed.
(Fred Perry)

If you think marriage is going to be perfect you're probably still at your reception. *(Martha Bolton)*

I love golf so much I played last week instead of attending a wedding. Mine. *(Joe O'Donovan)*

Statistics have proven that at least 50% of all the people who get married at Easter are women. *(George Coote)*

One of the most enjoyable weddings I was at was the one where the father of the bride had a heart attack during the soup course. We were profoundly grateful that the speeches were cancelled. *(David Slattery)*

I had a civil ceremony. His mother couldn't come.
(Phyllis Diller)

When John got a picture of my wedding to Linda he crossed out the word 'wedding' and put in 'funeral' instead.
(Paul McCartney on John Lennon)

It was not a happy day for me when I found out about a Yale University study saying that women not married by the age of 40 have a greater chance of being kidnapped by a terrorist than walking down the aisle to say 'I do'. *(Oprah Winfrey)*

If it were not for the presents, an elopement would be preferable.
    (George Ade)

At a wedding you never hear a man clearly say, 'I do'. We figure
    we can get out of it later on a technicality. *(Sinbad)*

I'll never forget my wedding day – much as I try.
    (Bob Monkhouse)

Let's be honest: a wedding is absolutely the worst day to start
    married life. *(Caitlin Moran)*

We had a quiet wedding. Her father had a silencer on the shotgun.
    (Sean Kilroy)

When I get invited to a wedding I always give the newlyweds a
    $50 voucher for a firm of solicitors I know. *(Jenny Éclair)*

I spent twenty grand on my daughter's wedding and they had
    the gall to say I gave her away. *(Dean Martin)*

Immediately after the ceremony, the bride and groom went into
    the vestry and sighed. *(Newspaper typo in Manchester News)*

I was sorry I couldn't go to my mother's fifth wedding but I
    promised her I'd be at her next one. *(Liza Minnelli)*

The terrible question which confronts all brides is whether to
    pin up their curls and cream their faces before going to bed.
    (Virginia Graham)

Clodagh and Pat have just ended a life-long friendship. They got
    married. *(Peter Cagney)*

Marrying Priest: 'Wilt thou have this woman to thy wedded wife?'
Groom: 'Oh, decisions, decisions!' *(The Golden Girls)*

Congratulations from all your friends at the Family Planning Center. P.S, The test is positive. *(Telegram once sent to a bewildered bride)*

This particular Paddy confesses that it was frightening for him to realise that at the very moment both people said, 'I do' he was transported from a sniveling, guilt-ridden, self-conscious, randy single man into a raving sex maniac with a game licence who was exhorted to procreate henceforth like bunnies in Ballybunion. *(Mick Doyle)*

My wife was a bag of nerves the day we got married. Now she's just a bag. *(Big O)*

When Barbra Streisand's husband looked at her face the first morning after the wedding he said, 'For Christ's sake, sing!' *(John Grossman)*

The most difficult years of marriage are those following the wedding. *(Bob Hope)*

The weddings I like best are the ones where I'm not getting married. *(Jimmy Logan)*

I only made one mistake in marriage: saying 'I do'. *(Gloria Swanson)*

My father was a keen trade unionist. He insisted on a tea break on his wedding night. *(Les Dawson)*

It doesn't really matter what you do on your stag night as long as the next morning the groom wakes up naked and handcuffed to an orangutan in a cage in the hold of a Boeing 747 which has just landed in Jakarta. *(Adrian Edmondson)*

Say Yes to the Dress

My mother puts on her wedding dress from time to time. Not
  because she's sentimental. She just gets really far behind with
  her laundry. *(Brian Kiley)*

A bride at her second wedding doesn't wear a veil. She wants to
  see what she's getting. *(Helen Rowland)*

Skimp on your wedding dress. Why spend a lot of money
  on something you're only going to wear five or six times?
  (Charisse Savarin)

The tuxedo is a wedding safety device created by women because
  they know that men are undependable. So in case the groom
  chickens out, everybody just takes one step over and the
  ceremony continues. *(Jerry Seinfeld)*

The reason wedding dresses are white is so they go with all the
  other household appliances. *(Mort Sahl)*

A woman will dress up to go shopping, water the plants,
  empty the garbage, answer the phone, read a book, get
  the mail. A man dresses up for weddings and funerals.
  (Matt Groening)

My wife thinks I should buy her a new dress just because she's
  fed up treading on the evil of the one she's got. *(Roy Brown)*

Young wives are very sentimental these days. They want to get
  divorced in the same dress their mother was divorced in.
  (Hal Roach)

Never trust anyone wearing a wedding dress, especially a woman.
(Ted Danson)

The bride, who was given away by her father, wore a dress
of white figured brocade with a trailing veil held in
place by a coronet of pearls. She carried a bouquet of
rosebuds and goods vehicles, leaving free access to all
private vehicles not built for more than seven passengers.
(Notice in Atherstone News and Herald)

A woman seldom asks advice until she has bought her
wedding clothes. *(Joseph Addison)*

The bride wore her grandmother's dress. Her grandmother
was freezing. *(Pam Ayres)*

A bridegroom's mother is supposed to wear beige and keep her
mouth shut. *(Erma Bombeck)*

A woman I know has been married so many times she has rice
marks on her face. She has a wash-and-wear bridal gown.
(Henny Youngman)

Love, Honour, Obey

I can't fall in love. That's probably what holds my
marriage together. *(Joseph Heller)*

My wife and I thought we were in love but it turned out
to be benign. *(Woody Allen)*

I fall in love really quickly and this scares guys away. I'm like,
'I'm in love with you. I want to marry you.' And they're like,
'Ma'am, could you give me ten bucks for the pizza and I'll be
outta here?' *(Penny Wiggins)*

Greater love than this no man hath but that he lays down his
wife for his friend. *(James Joyce)*

I was unlucky in love. My first two wives died and my
third one wouldn't. *(Bob Monkhouse)*

The only woman I ever loved left me and got married.
My mother. *(Emo Philips)*

If my wife really loved me she would have married someone else.
(Steve Martin)

I fell in love with her smile but married the rest of her too. Drat.
(W.C. Fields)

Love and marriage used to go together like a horse and carriage.
These days it's love and sex that go together. It's still possible
to have one without the other, but only if you join a religious
order. *(Guy Browning)*

It's bloody impractical to love, honour and obey. If it weren't, you wouldn't have to sign a contract. *(Katharine Hepburn)*

Marriage is when you go from swearing to love to loving to swear. *(Hal Roach)*

I recently read that love is a matter of chemistry. That must be why my wife treats me like toxic waste. *(David Bissonette)*

In their first passions women are in love with their lover; in all the rest, with love. *(Duc de la Rochefoucauld)*

I believe in love and marriage, but not necessarily with the same person. *(John Travolta)*

It's only better to have loved and lost if you have a good lawyer. *(Herb Caen)*

Love is a temporary insanity, often curable by marriage. *(Ambrose Bierce)*

I've been in love with the same woman for 41 years. If my wife finds out, she'll kill me. *(Henny Youngman)*

Half the marriages in Hollywood are like tennis: love means nothing. *(Jerry Colonna)*

Love and marriage go together like a horse and carnage. *(Erica Jong)*

With This Ring I Thee Wed

Marriage is something that puts a ring on a woman's finger and two under a man's eyes. *(Hal Roach)*

She: 'A ring is a symbol of love because it has no beginning and no end.'
He: 'Yeah, and there's a hole in the middle of it.'

I bought my girlfriend a lovely engagement ring for Christmas but she dropped it on the floor and the dog ate it. We've been going through the motions ever since. *(Frank Skinner)*

It's hot in here. I think I'll take my ring off. *(Fred Allen)*

He: 'You're wearing your wedding ring on the wrong finger.'
She: 'I know. I married the wrong man.'

If he isn't willing to wear a wedding ring but expects you to, head for Reno. *(Madonna)*

Never give back the ring. Never. Swallow it first. *(Joan Rivers)*

Harrison Ford proposed to Calista Flockhart by slipping an engagement ring around her waist. *(Rhona Cameron)*

My wife is really sentimental. One Valentine's Day I gave her a ring and to this day she's never forgotten those three little words that were engraved inside: 'Made in Taiwan'. *(Leopold Fechtner)*

Marriage involves three types of ring: engagement ring, wedding ring, suffer-ring. *(Don Rickles)*

For Richer, For Poorer

I spent so much on my girlfriend I decided to marry her
for my money. *(Richard Pryor)*

My wife didn't marry me for my money. She married me for my
father's money. *(Nicky Hilton)*

There's a way of transferring funds today that's even faster than
electronic banking. It's called marriage. *(Michael Jordan)*

The only sort of man most women want to marry is the fella
with a will of his own – preferably made out in her favour.
(Brendan Behan)

You say stupid things to the person you're in love with. Like,
'Here's all my money'. *(Sean Hughes)*

My marriage vows should have included the phrase, 'Till debt do
us part.' *(Kelly Smith)*

I like men who are prematurely wealthy. *(Joan Rivers)*

My marriage to Max Reed ended after the bastard tried to sell
me to a sheik for $20,000. *(Joan Collins)*

How marriage ruins a man. It's as demoralizing as cigarettes...
and far more expensive. *(Oscar Wilde)*

A successful man is one who makes more than his wife can spend.
A successful woman is someone who can find such a man.
(Lana Turner)

Most of the women in my family married for money but not
a lot of money. You can't go to a reading of a will in the
family without someone asking, 'Who's getting the tools?'
(Laura Kightlinger)

Mother told me a couple of years ago, 'Sweetheart, settle down
and marry a rich man.' I said, 'Mom, I *am* a rich man.' *(Cher)*

My ex-wife Joan Collins is a commodity who would sell her own
bowel movement. *(Anthony Newley)*

The greatest tragedy is to marry a man for love and then find out
he has no money. *(Zsa Zsa Gabor)*

All work and no play makes Jack's wife a rich widow.
(Tom McDermott)

She said to her fiancé, 'If you suddenly became very rich, would
you still love me?' He said, 'Of course, but I'd miss you
terribly.' *(Mort Sahl)*

The average wedding costs eighteen thousand quid. That's
everything out of the Argos catalogue right there. My advice?
Marry a Buddhist. They always want to get married under
a tree. 'No problem, love. Oak or larch? It's your big day.'
(Jeff Green)

I didn't marry my wife because she had £4 million. I would have
married her even if she only had £2 million. *(Charles Forte)*

Weddings have become so expensive these days it's the
father of the bride who breaks down and cries now.
(Paul Murtagh)

I only want a man who is kind and understanding. Is *zat* too much to ask of a millionaire? *(Zsa Zsa Gabor)*

Let Them Eat Cake

The marriage between Mack Gilbert and Melinda Marx
was so short, the bride got custody of the wedding cake.
(George Jessel)

Why did I marry three times? It was for a day out in the frock. I
really can't stand wedding cake. *(Julie Goodyear)*

Scientists have discovered a food that reduces a woman's sex
drive by 99%. Wedding cake. *(Jim Davidson)*

The greatest threat to Liz Taylor's diet plans was always
wedding cake. *(Mike Barfield)*

The wedding was so emotional, even the cake ended up in tiers.
(Fred Allen)

The Institution in a Nutshell

Marriage is a deal in which a man gives away half his groceries in
order to get the other half cooked. *(John Gwynne)*

Marriage is an outmoded convention started by cavemen and
continued by florists. *(Olivia de Havilland)*

Marriage is all right – but it's carrying love a bit too far.
(Texas Guinan)

Marriage is a good thing, and so is a bone for a dog.
But if you tie it to his tail it will drive him mad.
(Colonel George Hangar)

Marriage is lonelier than solitude. *(Beverley Sills)*

Marriage begins when you sink into his arms and ends with your
arms in his sink. *(Shelley Winters)*

Marriage is part of a sort of fifties revival package that's
back in vogue along with neckties and naked ambition.
(Calvin Trillin)

Marriage is an attempt to change a night owl into
a homing pigeon. *(Joey Bishop)*

Marriage is a long dull meal with the dessert at the beginning.
(Dean Martin)

Marriage is a ghastly public confession of a strictly
private intention. *(Ian Hay)*

They say marriages are made in heaven. So are thunder and
lightning. *(Clint Eastwood)*

Marriage is the waste paper basket of the emotions.
(Bertrand Russell)

Marriage is a bribe to make a housekeeper think she's
a house-holder. *(Thornton Wilder)*

Marriage is three parts love and seven parts forgiveness of sins.
(Langdon Mitchell)

Marriage is a state consisting of a master, a mistress and two
slaves, making in all, two. *(Ambrose Beirce)*

Marriage is neither heaven or hell – it is simply purgatory.
(Abraham Lincoln)

Marriage is three meals a day and remembering to
bring out the trash. *(Milton Berle)*

Marriage is a wonderful invention but then again so is the
bicycle repair kit. *(Billy Connolly)*

Marriage is bed and bored. *(George Saunders)*

Marriage is the process of discovering what kind of woman your
husband would have preferred. *(Natalie Wood)*

Marriage is the tomb of friendship. *(Richard Burton)*

Marriage is an attempt to solve problems with your wife that you
wouldn't have if you weren't married to her. *(Eddie Cantor)*

Marriage is when a woman asks a man to remove his
   pyjamas because she wants to send them to the laundry.
   (Albert Finney)

The medical term for a woman paralysed from the waist down
   and the neck up is 'Marriage'. *(Kathy Lette)*

Honeymoons

I was married in 1969. It was ten years before we could afford to go on our honeymoon. *(Paul Durcan)*

Nobody but a monumental bore would have thought of having a honeymoon at Budleigh Salterton. *(Noel Coward)*

At the honeymoon hotel the desk clerk said, 'Is this your most charming wife?' I said, 'No, it's the only one I've got.' *(Bud Abbott)*

My sex was so great during the honeymoon, even the guests in the next room had a cigarette afterwards. *(Don Rickles)*

Niagara Falls is the second biggest disappointment of the average honeymoon. *(Oscar Wilde)*

After our honeymoon I felt like a new man. The trouble was, my wife said she did too. *(Kevin Goldstein-Jackson)*

Next to hot chicken soup, a tattoo of an anchor on your chest and penicillin, I consider a honeymoon one of the most over-rated events in the world. *(Erma Bombeck)*

I never seemed to bring out the best in men. My third husband threw me out of the car on our honeymoon. *(Bette Davis)*

I was once engaged to a man who was very good to his mother. That impressed me. I was always told that a man will treat his wife like he treats his mother. We broke up when he told me he wanted to bring her on the honeymoon. *(Teresa Gaffney)*

The honeymoon is over when the dog brings you your slippers and your wife barks at you. *(Hugh Griffith)*

However perfect the honeymoon, the time will come when you wish she would fall downstairs and break a leg. *(Raymond Chandler)*

So Rod Stewart's getting married again. Where's he going to go on honeymoon – Viagra Falls? *(Gordon McDonald)*

The honeymoon wasn't such a ghastly experience really. It was afterwards that was really awful. *(Noel Coward)*

The honeymoon is over when she starts calling him 'Listen' instead of 'Honey.' *(Leopold Fechtner)*

Ever since the honeymoon ended, my wife has been hitting the ceiling. It's just as well she's such a lousy shot. *(Peter Cagney)*

He promised his fiancée the world, the moon and the stars. On their honeymoon he took her to the planetarium. *(Joey Adams)*

I knew a man who was so industrious he went on his honeymoon alone, leaving his wife at home to mind the shop. *(Jack Cruise)*

Home Sweet Home

There's a sign in the kitchen of our house which states, 'We interrupt this marriage to bring you the football season'. *(Gordon Strachan)*

I always bring my wife her tea in my pyjamas but she says she'd prefer to have it in a cup. *(Eric Morecambe)*

Throughout the whole of our marriage Dylan never spent a single evening at home. *(Caitlin Thomas)*

The main advantage marriage offers to women is someone to hold the stepladder while they paint the kitchen ceiling. *(Fran Lebowitz)*

Housework is so boring. You make the beds, clean the floors and do the dishes and then six months later you have to do it all over again. *(Rosaleen Linehan)*

Marriage is the best magician there is. In front of your eyes it can change an exciting, cute little dish into a boring dish-washer. *(Jerry Lewis)*

A decent husband is someone who'll lift his legs up from the sofa while his wife is doing the hoovering. *(Dan Bennett)*

One of the best things about marriage is that it gets young people to bed at a decent hour. *(M.M. Musselman)*

Home is where you can say anything you like because nobody listens to you anyway. *(Billy Connolly)*

After seven years of marriage I'm sure of two things. First, never wallpaper together. And second, you'll need two bedrooms – both for her. *(Dennis Miller)*

I burned a lot of my ironing in the backyard. *(Phyllis Diller)*

My wife is an interior decorator. She wants to get rid of me because I clash with the curtains. *(Morey Amsterdam)*

My husband hasn't mowed the front lawn in so long, the only way the postman can get to the front door is to swing on a vine. *(Peg Bracken)*

The man at the door was trying to sell my wife washing-up liquid. 'All it takes is a little squirt,' he said. 'It's okay,' she told him, 'I already have one.' *(Ronnie Corbett)*

My wife is afraid to leave dirty dishes in the sink. She's worried a burglar will break in and be disgusted. *(Sam Levenson)*

My husband is so lazy, when I asked him to buy a 'Do it Yourself' book he got me to read it to him. *(Phyllis Diller)*

I don't like to be called 'Housewife.' I prefer 'Domestic Goddess.' *(Roseanne)*

I'm an ordinary sort of fellow – 42 around the chest, 42 around the waist, 96 around the golf course and a nuisance around the house. *(Groucho Marx)*

My wife has a new super new high-powered hair dryer. Yesterday she dried her hair in ten seconds. But now her eyebrows are missing. *(Gene Perret)*

My wife gets mixed up with all the gadgets in the kitchen. Yesterday she tried to defrost the stove. *(Milton Berle)*

My wife said her wildest sexual fantasy would be if I got my own apartment. *(Rodney Dangerfield)*

I don't go out on any more bad dates. I'd rather be home alone than out with some guy who sells socks on the internet. *(Miranda Hobbes)*

I married at 21. It was just an excuse to get out of the house. *(David Letterman)*

I come from a broken home. I broke it. *(Roy Brown)*

Throughout our marriage my wife has always stood by me. She has to. We've only got one chair. *(Tommy Cooper)*

How often does a house need to be cleaned? Just once every wife. *(Stan Fuller)*

The honeymoon is over when he wants the kitchen in good shape rather than a good shape in the kitchen. *(Red Skelton)*

The most popular labour-saving device is still a husband with money. *(Joey Adam)*

I was cleaning out the attic the other day with the wife. Filthy, dirty and covered with cobwebs. But she's good with kids. *(Tommy Cooper)*

Our new juicer makes juice from anything. Last week my wife gave me a glass of toast. *(Ernie Kovacs)*

I miss my wife's cooking – as often as I can. *(Henny Youngman)*

My husband expects me to know where everything is, as if the uterus is a tracking device. *(Roseanne)*

My husband's had liposuction. That's the last time he'll ask me to do the hoovering! *(Jo Brand)*

While re-decorating, I realized my wife and I had radically different ideas on furniture. She wanted to keep pieces that reflected the French provincial theme she was creating whereas I wanted to keep all the stuff we'd had sex on. *(Brad Osberg)*

Don't cook or clean. No man will ever make love to a woman because she waxed the linoleum. 'My God, the floor's immaculate. Lie down, you hot bitch.' *(Joan Rivers)*

You can tell a husband isn't handy when he asks the next door neighbour how to get blood off a saw. *(Phyllis Diller)*

Have you noticed how women whose marriages are breaking up keep re-decorating the kitchen? *(Matthew Paris)*

I was married to a capitalist and a communist and neither of them would take out the trash. *(Zsa Zsa Gabor)*

Bride and Prejudice

Wives are like cockroaches. They'll survive after a nuclear attack.
(Lorrie Moore)

The ideal wife for an Irishman is a rich dumb blonde nymphomaniac who owns a pub near a racecourse and turns into a pizza after sex. *(Sean Kilroy)*

My wife has a very even disposition: she's miserable all the time.
(Henny Youngman)

Wives are young men's mistresses, companions for middle age and old men's nurses. *(Frances Bacon)*

My wife isn't so smart. She has to reach into her bra to count to two. *(Tommy Dempsey)*

I got a lovely dog for my wife. It was a great swap.
(Bob Monkhouse)

Basically my wife was immature. I'd be at home in my bath and she'd come in and sink my boats. *(Woody Allen)*

My wife has faith in me as a comedian and lover – I just wish she'd remember when to stop laughing. *(Bob Hope)*

Stan Waltz has decided to take unto himself a wife. But he hasn't yet decided whose. *(Peter De Vries)*

'WIFE' stands for 'Washing', Ironing, Fucking, Etc.'
(Kathy Lette)

If wives were good, God would have had one. *(Georgian proverb)*

My wife kisses the dog on the lips but she won't drink from my glass. *(Rodney Dangerfield)*

A wife only lasts for the length of a marriage but an ex-wife is there for the rest of your life. *(Woody Allen)*

My first marriage didn't put me off women – just women like my first wife. *(Bob Hoskins)*

A wife is worse than a tennis coach. At least the coach goes home in the evening. *(Ilie Nastase)*

I'm not saying my wife is cold but when she opens her mouth a light comes on. *(Joe Cuddy)*

A wife laughs at her husband's jokes not because they're clever but because she is. *(Leopold Fechtner)*

Spanish has the same word for handcuffs and wives. Go figure. *(Howard Marks)*

I should have known something was wrong with my first wife when I brought her home to meet my parents and they approved. *(Woody Allen)*

I can' t find any thread of consistency in my marriages. My wives were a mixed bag: a schoolgirl, a gentlewoman, an actress, a ballerina... and a crocodile. *(John Huston)*

My wife is on a diet of coconuts and bananas. She hasn't lost any weight but she can sure climb a tree. *(Henny Youngman)*

Every man needs a wife because there are some things he can't blame on the government. *(George Burns)*

Mistresses get a steady diet of whipped cream but no meat and potatoes: wives get the reverse. *(Merle Shain)*

There's no fury like an ex-wife searching for a new lover. *(Cyril Connolly)*

I've never regretted a moment of life with my wife. She's beautiful. She's gorgeous. She's listening. *(Brendan O'Carroll)*

America is the land of permanent waves and impermanent wives. *(Brendan Behan)*

What everybody needs in the music industry is a wife. I wish I had a wife. *(Chrissie Hynde)*

The cave-dweller's wife complained to her husband that he hadn't dragged her anywhere in months. *(Laurence Peter)*

Every now and then I do something that annoys my wife. Like breathing. *(Bob Monkhouse)*

Wives are people who think it's against the law not to answer the phone when it rings. *(Ring Lardner)*

I met my wife under unfortunate circumstances. I was single. *(Sean Rafferty)*

What's Left of the Lover

A husband is what's left of the lover after the nerve has been extracted. *(Helen Rowland)*

My first husband used to run in the door, throw his arms around me...and tell me how wonderful he was. *(Shelley Winters)*

I asked my husband to restore my confidence. I told him my boobs were gone, my stomach was gone. I asked him to say something nice about my legs. 'Blue goes with everything', he said. *(Joan Rivers)*

The only thing my husband and I have in common is that we were married on the same day. *(Phyllis Diller)*

There's so little difference between husbands you might as well keep the first one. *(Adela Rogers St. John)*

My husband is so stupid he thinks a crap game is where people take bets on who can throw dried cow droppings the farthest. *(Joan Rivers)*

My ex-husband said someday he'd go far. I said, 'I hope you stay there.' *(Drew Barrymore)*

My husband always felt marriage and a career didn't mix. That's why he's never worked. *(Phyllis Diller)*

Woman 1: 'I don't know what to make of my husband.'
Woman 2: 'How about mincemeat?'
   (Seamus O'Leary)

My husband has so many faults, his nickname is San Andreas.
(Kirstie Alley)

A woman once put an ad in the Classifieds saying, 'Husband wanted.'
The next day she received a hundred letters. They all said the
same thing: 'You can have mine.' *(John Scally)*

I never speak of my ex-husbands except under hypnosis.
(Joan Collins)

The only thing my husband ever achieved on his own is his
moustache. *(Constance Bennett)*

A husband is just as hard to find after marriage as before it.
(Kathleen Behan)

The worst thing about being married is having a husband. *(Roseanne)*

My ex-husband was so far up hi ass, he could polish his ulcers.
(Hermione Gingold)

My first husband and I lived happily never after. *(Bette Davis)*

I had a love-hate relationship with one of my husbands. He loved me
and I hated him. *(Zsa Zsa Gabor)*

Married men make the worst husbands. *(Lily Tomlin)*

When my husband was born it wasn't a stork that delivered him. It
was a vulture. *(Roseanne)*

I've just found the perfect husband. It's a pity I'm not married to him.
(Judy Tenuta)

Mothers-in-Law

Murphy kept a photograph of his mother-in-law above the
fireplace. He said it kept the children away from the fire.
(Hal Roach)

I saw six men punching and kicking the mother-in-law. My
neighbour said, 'Are you not going to help?' I said, 'No, six
should be enough'. *(Les Dawson)*

The awe and dread with which the untutored savage
contemplates his mother-in-law are amongst the most
familiar facts of anthropology. *(George Frazer)*

My wife said, 'Can my mother come down for the weekend?' I
said 'Why?' She said, 'Two weeks is far too long to leave
anyone on the roof'. *(Bob Monkhouse)*

My mother-in-law has a disgusting habit. She comes to visit me.
(Des MacHale)

I'm not saying my mother-in-law is tough but when she eats
sardines she doesn't bother to open the tin. *(Des MacHale)*

When I got married my mother-in-law said the bride and I made
a lovely couple except for me. *(George Burns)*

My wife's mother was less distressed by losing her daughter than
by the fact that when I knelt at the altar rails she spotted a
hole in the sole of one of my shoes. *(Jack Hawkins)*

Mothers-in-law belong to the meddle classes. *(Jim Davidson)*

I never forget a face but in my mother-in-law's case I'm willing to
make an exception. *(Groucho Marx)*

I left my wife because of another woman. Her mother.
(Gene Perret)

A mother-in-law dies when another devil is needed in hell.
(Sean Kilroy)

The ultimate penalty for bigamy is two mothers-in-law.
(George Russell)

The mother-in-law must be at the door. The mice are throwing
themselves into the traps. *(Roy Brown)*

Mixed emotion is watching your mother-in-law drive over a cliff
in your new Ferrari. *(Long John Lebel)*

When it comes to broken marriages, most husbands will split
the blame – half his wife's fault and half her mother's.
(Rodney Dangerfield)

My mother-in-law has come round to our house for Christmas
seven years running but this year we're having a change.
We're letting her in. *(Les Dawson)*

Adam was the luckiest man in history: he had no mother-in-law.
(Sholem Alacheim)

I heard of a mother-in-law who went to Sydney for a holiday.
While swimming on Bondi beach she was attacked by a great
white shark. The doctors worked all night but it was no
good. The shark died. *(Hal Roach)*

Behind every successful man stands a surprised mother-in-law. *(Hubert Humphrey)*

I've just got back from a pleasure trip. I took my mother-in-law to the airport. *(Les Dawson)*

My mother-in-law is on holiday so to make up I have a woman come in and nag me three days a week. *(Henny Youngman)*

English law prohibits a man from marrying his mother-in-law. This is a perfect example of totally unnecessary litigation. *(Somerset Maugham)*

Doolan: 'I want some arsenic for my mother-in-law.'
Chemist: 'Have you a prescription?'
Doolan: 'No, but here's her picture.'
(Hal Roach)

Be kind to your mother-in-law. Babysitters are expensive. *(Leopold Fechtner)*

It's not that we didn't get along; it's just that my mother-in-law is very objective. She objected to everything I did. *(Beverly d'Angelo)*

My mother-in-law has just vanished. I'd give a description of her to the police but they wouldn't believe me. *(Les Dawson)*

Why Get Married?

I wanted to marry her from the moment I saw the moonlight shining on the barrel of her father's shotgun. *(Eddie Albert)*

If I ever marry it will be on a sudden impulse, as when a man shoots himself. *(H.L. Mencken)*

My ambition is to marry a rich girl who's too proud to let her husband work. *(Leopold Fechtner)*

I'd marry a midget just for the handicapped parking. *(Kathleen Madigan)*

I'd like to get married because I like the idea of a man being required by law to sleep with me every night. *(Carrie Snow)*

My marriage was my dad's idea. She was the girl next door and her father had an electric drill. *(Ronnie Corbett)*

I'm going to marry a virgin. I can't stand criticism. *(Mitch Miller)*

It was so cold in London one year I almost got married. *(Shelley Winters)*

She married a sailor because she wanted to have children and rear admirals. *(Peter Cagney)*

I got fed up being turned down my birds in the pub. *(Eric Clapton on why he got married in 1979)*

He married her to get rid of her. *(Sian Phillips)*

Most people get married because they're hopelessly in love. After that it's a toss-up which lasts longer – the love or the hopelessness. *(Terry Martin)*

There was a glorious era in my life during which my contemporaries went one by one to the altar with the ecstatic insouciance of a Versailles under-chef heading for the guillotine. *(Hugh Leonard)*

The trouble about women is that they get all excited about nothing and then marry it. *(Cher)*

My daughter overlooked a lot of things in her fiancé. He was on probation for a marijuana arrest and a DUI. The honeymoon was house arrest. I think he married her for a designated driver. *(Daryl Hogue)*

I'm a great believer in the institution of marriage and can hardly wait to get married myself. In fact I intend to do so as often as possible. Not that I'm a romantic or anything. It's just that if I'm going to get fat, disillusioned and sad anyway, I'm bloody well taking somebody with me. *(Joe O'Connor)*

He married a woman to stop her getting away./Now she's there all day. *(Philip Larkin)*

A man marries to have a home, but also because he doesn't want to be bothered with sex and all that sort of thing. *(Somerset Maugham)*

I got married because I was tired of going to the launderette, eating take-away food all the time and always having holes in my socks. I got divorced for the same reasons. *(Fred Metcalf)*

Why did I marry Artie Shaw? Everyone married Artie Shaw!
　(Ava Gardner)

I told my father I had half a mind to get married. He said that
　was all I needed. *(Roy Brown)*

Most men flirt with the women they would not marry
　and marry the women who would not flirt with them.
　(Jackie Mason)

He tricked me into marrying him. He told me I was pregnant.
　(Carol Liefer)

The Long and Short of Marriage

My parents stayed together for forty years, but mainly out of spite. *(Woody Allen)*

I'd like to get married again but I'm afraid of the commitment. I mean, we're talking two, maybe even three years of my life here. *(Maura Kennedy)*

I was once married for 29 days, which was about 28 days too long. *(Drew Barrymore on her 1994 marriage to Jeremy Thomas)*

Imagine spending eternity with the same woman. Even if she was the greatest bonk in the world you'd get bored after the first 900,000 years. *(Ozzy Osbourne)*

I've been married six months. She looks like a million dollars but she only knows 120 words and she's only got two ideas in her head. The other one's hats. *(Eric Linklater)*

Jack Nicholson and my daughter lived together for twelve years. That's longer than any of my marriages lasted. *(John Huston)*

Some people ask the secret of our long marriage. It's like this: we both go to a restaurant two times a week. A little candle-light, dinner, soft music and dancing. She goes Tuesdays, I go Fridays. *(Henny Youngman)*

Marriage means you study one another for three weeks, love each other for three months, fight for three years... and tolerate the situation for thirty. *(Andre de Missan)*

I've been married a while. You know you've become too
   dependent on your husband when you ask him to scratch an
   itch you can reach yourself. *(Roberta Rockwell)*

My first marriage lasted five minutes. No, wait – four.
   (Maureen O'Hara)

I've been married so long I'm on my third bottle of Tabasco.
   (Susan Vass)

I've had diseases that lasted longer than my marriages. *(Neil Carter)*

My husband and myself are in what some call the 'nesting' stage
   of marriage. It's like, 'The sex is getting boring so let's buy
   some furniture.' *(Christine Blackburn)*

Marriage is forever – with time off for bad behaviour.
   (Robert Downey Jr)

I'm afraid of marriage because you have to make love to the
   same person for, like 300 years. How do you keep it exciting?
   Hats? *(Elayne Boosler)*

Marriage is for life, which these days can mean sixty or more years.
   A good way to fill in the time is by having six or seven children.
   This gives you something to do for the long middle years in a
   marriage when there's nothing on television. *(Guy Browning)*

And they said the marriage wouldn't last. Well they left the
   church together, didn't they? *(Mel Brooks)*

You may marry the man of your dreams, ladies, but fourteen
   years later you're looking at a couch that burps. *(Roseanne)*

Rumpling the Bedclothes

Sex is bad because it rumples the bedclothes. *(Jacqueline Onassis)*

Sex is for men. Marriage, like lifeboats, is for women and children. *(Carrie Fisher)*

Sex in marriage? It doesn't happen. After you say 'I do', you don't. *(Michael Harkness)*

My wife insists on turning off the lights when we make love. That's not so bad. But then she hides. *(Les Dawson)*

I know nothing about sex because I was always married. *(Zsa Zsa Gabor)*

Sex in marriage is like medicine. Three times a day for the first week, once a day for another week, then once every three or four days until the condition clears up. *(Peter de Vries)*

This is God's cruel joke: By the time men figure out what women want in bed, their penis doesn't work anymore. *(Bill Hicks)*

I could never have sex with any woman who didn't respect my wife. *(Dan Greenberg)*

The only reason my wife has an orgasm is so she'll have something else to moan about. *(Bob Monkhouse)*

The other night I was making love to my wife and she said, 'Deeper, deeper!' So I started quoting Nietzsche to her. *(Dennis Miller)*

It was the perfect Irish marriage. She didn't want to and he couldn't. *(Spike Milligan)*

I asked my wife, 'On a scale of one to ten, how do you rate me as a lover?' She said, 'Come on – you know I'm no good at fractions.' *(Rodney Dangerfield)*

He: 'I want to make love to you badly.'
She: 'You always do.'

Nothing happened in our marriage. I nicknamed the waterbed Lake Placid. *(Phyllis Diller)*

My sex life is now reduced to fan letters from an elderly lesbian who wants to borrow $800. *(Groucho Marx in 1974)*

I never really had a childhood. When I was eight my favourite book was 'Everything You Always Wanted to Know About Sex But Were Afraid to Ask'. I was not afraid to ask. *(Drew Barrymore)*

My wife doesn't. Understand me? *(Idris Humphreys)*

Marriage is the price men pay for sex and sex is the price women pay for marriage. *(Alan Bennett)*

My wife screams when she's having sex. Especially when I walk in on her. *(Roy Brown)*

I remember the first time I had sex. I still have the receipt. *(Groucho Marx)*

My wife gives good headache. *(Rodney Dangerfield)*

My husband committed suicide because I took the bag off my
head when we were making love. *(Joan Rivers)*

Do I believe in sex before marriage? Sure, so long as it doesn't
delay the ceremony. *(Milton Berle)*

When my wife has sex with me there's always a reason. One
night she used me to time an egg. *(Rodney Dangerfield)*

The best way to keep a man from pestering you for sex is to
marry him. *(Phyllis Diller)*

My wife is a sex object. Every time I ask her for sex, she objects.
(Les Dawson)

I'll give you some idea of my sex life with my first wife. She got
divorced in white. *(Bob Monkhouse)*

I don't see much of Alfred any more since he got so interested
in sex. *(Clara Kinsey on her famous husband)*

My husband makes love to me almost every day of the week
– almost Monday, almost Tuesday, almost Wednesday...
(Ruth Berle)

Husbands seem to think that 'Mutual Orgasm' is an insurance
company. *(Kathy Lette)*

If sex is the most fun you can have with your clothes off, divorce
is the least fun you can have with them on. *(David Quantick)*

A woman should behave like a cook in the kitchen and a whore
in the bedroom. *(Oliver Reed)*

The trouble with my wife is that she's a whore in the kitchen and
a cook in the bedroom. *(Geoffrey Gorer)*

In India a farmhand was caught in a sexual act with a cow.
He said he had bad eyesight and thought it was his wife.
(Spike Milligan)

And Baby Makes Three

I asked my mother if I was adopted. 'Not yet,' she said, 'but we did place an ad.' *(Dana Snow)*

In my last stage of labour I threatened to take my husband to court for concealing a lethal weapon in his boxer shorts. *(Linda Fiterman)*

I want a child very badly. Do you know anybody? *(Dianne Wiest)*

My wife just told me the good news: I'm going to be a dad for the first time. The bad news is, we already have two kids. *(Brian Kiley)*

I want my children to have all the things I could never afford and then I want to move in with them. *(Steve Martin)*

Childbearing is hereditary. If your parents didn't have any children, you won't either. *(Jimmy O'Dea)*

My mother had morning sickness *after* I was born. *(Jackie Mason)*

A friend of mine confused her valium and her birth control pills. She had fifteen kids but didn't give a shit. *(Joan Rivers)*

Father on phone to nurse in hospital: 'Could I speak to my wife? She's just had a baby.'
Nurse: 'Is this her first child?'
Father: 'No, this is her husband.'
(Shaun Connors)

I subscribe to the Evelyn Waugh School of fatherhood. The chap
buggers off to Abyssinia and then sends a telegram saying.
'Have you had our child yet and what have you called it?'
(Bob Geldof)

My unhealthy affection for my second daughter had waned.
Now I despise all my seven children equally. *(Evelyn Waugh)*

I planned on having one husband and seven children but it
turned out the other way around. *(Lana Turner)*

One thing they never tell you about child raising is that for the
rest of your life, at the drop of a hat, you're expected to know
your child's name and how old he or she is. *(Erma Bombeck)*

When I had my baby I screamed and screamed. And that was
just during the conception. *(Joan Rivers)*

'Suffer the little children to come unto me.' You'd know Jesus
wasn't married. *(Alan Bennett)*

In modern families the children don't live at home until after
they're married. *(Rosaleen Linehan)*

I've got seven kids. The three expressions you hear most
around my house are 'Hello', 'Goodbye' and 'I'm pregnant'.
(Dean Martin)

I'm not the world's best cook. I always threatened my children
with, 'If you don't shape up, you got to bed with dinner.'
(Erma Bombeck)

Children should be seen and not smelt. *(Joyce Jillson)*

A woman should never give birth after 35. 35 is enough kids for anyone. *(Gracie Allen)*

Don't tell your kids you had an easy birth or they won't respect you. For years I used to wake up my daughter and say, 'Melissa, you ripped me to shreds. Now go back to sleep.' *(Joan Rivers)*

The main reason children brighten a home is because they never turn off the bloody lights. *(Harry Secombe)*

In America there are two classes of travel: first class, and with children. *(Robert Benchley)*

Adults are always asking little kids what they want to be when they grow up – they're obviously looking for ideas. *(Paula Poundstone)*

I'm married to Beatrice Salkeld, a painter. We have no children except me. *(Brendan Behan)*

Be nice to your children. They're the ones who'll choose your nursing home. *(Cyril Connolly)*

A psychiatrist said, 'Be careful in the way you discipline your children or you could permanently damage their Id. Damage it? I didn't even know where it was. For all I knew, it either made you sterile or caused dandruff. Once I suspected where it was I made the kid wear four diapers just to be safe. *(Erma Bombeck)*

The mother of the year should be a sterilised woman with two adopted children. *(Paul Ehrlich)*

Few misfortunes can befall a boy which bring worse
consequences than to have a really affectionate mother.
(W. Somerset Maugham)

The best way to give advice to your kids is to find out what they
want and tell them to do it. *(Harry Truman)*

Never raise your hand to your children – it leaves your mid-
section unprotected. *(Robert Orpen)*

If you can't afford suppositories for your kids, a good cure for
constipation is to sit them on the lavvy and tell them ghost
stories. *(Roy 'Chubby' Brown)*

More twins are being born these days because babies are afraid to
come into the world alone. *(Herbert Prochnow)*

Everybody knows how to raise children except the people who
have them. *(PJ O'Rourke)*

To be a successful father there's one absolute rule: when
you have a kid, don't look at it for the first two years.
(Ernest Hemingway)

Children today only know two words: 'No' and 'Wallet'.
(Jasper Carrott)

Our son kept our marriage together. Neither of us wanted
custody of him. *(Roy 'Chubby' Brown)*

There are only two things a child will share willingly
– communicable diseases and his mother's age.
(Benjamin Spock)

I asked my old man if I could go ice-skating on the lake. He said, 'Wait till it gets warmer'. *(Rodney Dangerfield)*

My mother loved children. She would have given anything for me to be one. *(Groucho Marx)*

Because of their size, parents are very difficult to discipline. *(PJ O'Rourke)*

The only way to stop children from nagging to be taken to Disneyland is either to go or strangle them. *(Jeff Coren)*

One of the things I've discovered about children is that they don't really give a damn about the fact that you walked five miles to school. *(Patty Duke)*

With the birth of each child you lose two novels. *(Candida McWilliam)*

The next time I'm not just having an epidural for the birth – I'm having one for the conception as well. *(Sally James)*

Remember that as a teenager you're at the last stage in your life when you'll be happy to hear the phone is for you. *(Fran Lebowitz)*

I wasn't loved as a child. One day my mother said to me, 'Why can't you be more like Sheila?' Sheila died at birth. *(Joan Rivers)*

Do not, on a rainy day, ask your child what he feels like doing, because I can assure you that it is not something you'll feel like watching. *(Fran Lebowitz)*

Anyone who hates children and animals can't be all bad.
(W C Fields)

A teenager is an old person with sixty years deducted.
(Pat Ingoldsby)

The main trouble with children is that they're not returnable.
(Quentin Crisp)

All women become like their mothers. That is their tragedy. No man does. That's his. *(Oscar Wilde)*

It's no wonder people are so horrible when we consider the fact that they started life as children. *(Kingsley Amis)*

It's not the stork in the morning that brings the babies – it's the lark at night. *(Herbert Prochnow)*

There are three ways to get something done – do it yourself, hire someone, or forbid your kids to do it. *(Monta Crane)*

You can tell a child is growing up when he stops asking where he came from and refuses to say where he's going. *(Joan O'Donoghue)*

The best time to put children to bed is whenever they go. *(Joyce Jillson)*

My husband and I have discovered a foolproof method of birth control: an hour with the kids before bedtime. *(Roseanne)*

Do not allow your children to mix drinks. It's unseemly – and they use too much vermouth. *(Fran Lebowitz)*

It puzzles me how a child can see a dairy bar 3 miles away but can't see a 4 by 6 rug that's scrunched up under his feet and has been dragged through two rooms. *(Erma Bombeck)*

Cleaning your house while the kids are growing is like shoveling the walk before it stops snowing. *(Phyllis Diller)*

The best thing that could happen to motherhood already has: fewer women are going into it. *(Victoria Billings)*

My children never forgave me. Oedipus killed his father and married his mother, but I sold their Nintendo. *(Sue Arnold)*

Having a baby is like trying to push a grand piano through a transom. *(Alice Roosevelt Longworth)*

I knew I was an unwanted child when I saw that my new bath toys were a toaster and a radio. *(Joan Rivers)*

I'm a virgin and I brought up all my children to be the same. *(Shirley Bassey)*

Don't bother discussing sex with small children. They rarely have anything to add. *(Fran Lebowitz)*

A man in a delivery room is about as helpful as a nun at a bar mitzvah. *(Rita Rudner)*

The best way to keep children in the house is to create a harmonious atmosphere – and let the air out of their car tyres. *(Dorothy Parker)*

I lived in a normal family: I had no love for my father. *(Joe Orton)*

If one is not going to take the necessary precautions to avoid
    having parents, one must undertake to bring them up.
    (Quentin Crisp)

It's all any reasonable child can expect if the dad is present
    at the conception. *(Joe Orton)*

Setting a good example for your child takes all the fun out of
    middle age. *(William Faulkner)*

My mother never saw the irony in calling me a son of a bitch.
    (Jack Nicholson)

The modern child, when asked what he learned at school,
    replies, 'Nothing, but I gained some meaningful insights.'
    (Bill Vaughan)

Far better to have loved and lost than to have to buy shoes for
    eight kids. *(William Walton)*

The main trouble with children is that they're not returnable.
    (Quentin Crisp)

I don't like the little bastards. I like to hear the patter of little
    feet going away from me – especially two houses away.
    (Raymond Chandler)

We had a quicksand box in our backyard, I was an
    only child, eventually. *(Steven Wright)*

There's a time when you have to explain to your children why
    they're born – and it's a marvellous thing if you know the
    reason by then. *(Hazel Scott)*

I've got two wonderful children. Well, two out of five ain't bad.
   (Henny Youngman)

Insanity is hereditary: you get it from your children. *(Hal Roach)*

Any man who hates little children and small dogs can't be all bad.
   (W.C. Fields)

Children are a great comfort in your old age. They also help you
   to reach it faster. *(Lionel Kauffman)*

Many people prefer children to dogs. Principally, I
   think, because a licence is not required for the former.
   (Harry Graham)

There is much to be learnt from that piece of advice printed on
   most bottles of patent medicine: 'Keep Away From Small
   Children'. In fact I always have. *(Denis Norden)*

Setting a good example for your children takes all the fun out of
   middle age. *(William Feather)*

The first half of our lives is ruined by our parents and the second
   half by our children. *(Clarence Darrow)*

I hate babies. They remind me too much of monkeys. *(Saki)*

We've had bad luck with our kids – they've all grown up.
   (Christopher Morley)

Why do grandparents and grandchildren get along so
   well? Because they have the same enemy – the mother.
   (Claudette Colbert)

The real menace in dealing with a five-year-old is that in no time at all you begin to sound like a five-year-old. *(Jean Kerr)*

Be kind to your kids – don't have any. *(Graffito)*

Get revenge on your kids: live long enough to be a burden to them. *(Graffito)*

A food isn't necessarily healthy just because your child hates it. *(Katherine Whitehorn)*

A man finds out what is meant by a spitting image when he tries to feed cereal to his infant. *(Imogene Fey)*

I got so much food spat back in my face when my kids were small, I put windshield wipers on my glasses. *(Erma Bombeck)*

There's nothing worse than a man with a cold. He thinks he's dying. I always wonder how they'd survive childbirth. *(Miriam O'Callaghan)*

How do I cope with my children? I have a big house ... and I hide a lot. *(Mary Ure)*

Arguing the Toss

The best part of married life is the fights. The rest is merely so-so. *(Thornton Wilder)*

My wife loves to argue. When I said 'I Do', she said, 'Oh no you don't.' *(Terry Martin)*

You can't stay with a person you can't yell at. *(Erica Jong)*

Marriage is wonderful. It prevents husbands and wives picking fights with strangers. *(Jack Benny)*

A dentist got married to a manicurist. They fought tooth and nail. *(Tommy Cooper)*

My wife and I don't squabble or have rows. We're in an arms race, storing up warheads for a domestic Armageddon. *(Hugh Leonard)*

The calmest husbands make the stormiest wives. *(Isaac d'Israeli)*

The other night I had an argument with the dog. My wife said the dog was right. Now he has no respect for me. When my wife throws the ball, he waits for me to bring it back. *(Rodney Dangerfield)*

If you're married, it only takes one to make a quarrel. *(Ogden Nash)*

My wife and I keep arguing about sex and money. Personally I think she charges me too much. *(Rodney Dangerfield)*

When I arrived for work this morning my secretary said, 'I see you've had another quarrel with your wife.' I said, 'How did you know that?' She said, 'The kitchen knife is still stuck in your back.' *(Kevin Goldstein-Jackson)*

Never argue with your wife. It's just your word against hundreds of hers. *(Jack Benny)*

The problems never started in bed. We were always great in the bedroom. The problems started on the way to the bidet. *(Ava Gardner on her marriage to Frank Sinatra)*

My parents only had one argument in 45 years. It lasted for 43 of them. *(Cathy Ladman)*

A married couple are well suited when both partners feel the need for a quarrel at the same time. *(Jean Rostand)*

My wife and I had a rather interesting argument last night. She said it was five days since our last fight and I said it was four. *(Robert Orben)*

My wife and I have a great way of settling arguments. I admit I'm wrong and she admits she's right. *(Jack Benny)*

It's better to be quarrelling than lonely. *(Brendan Behan)*

A husband said to his wife, 'I don't know why you wear a bra, you've got nothing to put in it.' She replied, 'You wear briefs, don't you? *(Dawn French)*

I don't worry about terrorism. I was married for two years. *(Sam Kinison)*

There's only one difference between a wife and a terrorist. You can negotiate with a terrorist. *(Frank Carson)*

Marital Advice

Never marry an actor. They perform in every room in the
house except the boudoir – unless there's a mirror in there.
(Brigitte Bardot)

I told my daughter to get married, have a child, get divorced and
live happily ever after. *(Cher)*

If the bridegroom doesn't show up, marry the best man. After
a few weeks you won't notice the difference anyway.
(Helen Rowland)

Love your husband. Trust your husband. But get everything in
your own name. *(Joan Rivers)*

Men, take my advice and marry an orphan. First of all, there are
never any in-law problems. Second, there are no annoying
Thanksgiving and Christmas visits sitting around pretending
to enjoy the company of a couple of fifth-generation nitwits.
In fact when it comes to visiting her folks, the worst thing
that might happen to you would be an occasional trip to the
cemetery to leave some cheap flowers. *(George Carlin)*

Marry an archaeologist. The older you get, the more interested
he is in you. *(Agatha Christie)*

I don't go with feminism. My advice to women is to marry a
rich guy with a bad heart, then creep up behind him and say,
'Boo!' *(Joan Rivers)*

If you're afraid of loneliness, don't marry. *(Anton Chekhov)*

My father always said, 'Be the kind they marry, not the kind they date'. So on our first date I'd nag the guy for a dishwasher. *(Kris McGaha)*

Every man should have a wife – preferably his own. *(Zsa Zsa Gabor)*

Never ask your wife if she still hears from her old pimp. *(Johnny Carson)*

Whenever you want to marry someone, go have lunch with his ex-wife. *(Shelley Winters)*

If you make your husband feel important you'll have a happy and wonderful marriage – like two out of every ten couples. *(Mildred Natwick)*

My dad said, 'Marry a girl with the same beliefs as the family'. I thought: Why should I marry a girl who thinks I'm a schmuck? *(Adam Sandler)*

When a man steals your wife, there is no better revenge than to let him keep her. *(Sacha Guitry)*

To have a happy marriage, tell your spouse everything – except the essentials. *(Cynthia Nelms)*

Don't wear mascara if you're in love with a married man. *(Shirley MacLaine)*

The only thing that holds a marriage together is the husband being big enough to step back and see where his wife went wrong. *(Archie Bunker)*

I believe in large families. Every woman should have at least three husbands. *(Zsa Zsa Gabor)*

The best way to get your husband to do something is to suggest he's too old to do it. *(Ann Bancroft)*

The dread of loneliness is greater than the fear of bondage so get married. *(Cyril Connolly)*

Don't put all our eggs in one bastard. *(Dorothy Parker)*

Down with marriage – be a bachelor like your father was! *(Spike Milligan)*

Before criticizing your wife's faults, pause to consider they might have prevented her marrying someone better than you. *(Brendan Grace)*

Every woman should marry – and no man. *(Benjamin Disraeli)*

No man should have a secret from his wife. She invariably finds out. *(Oscar Wilde)*

Never marry a man with a big head. You're going to give birth to his child. You want a baby with a narrow head. *(Jilly Golden)*

If you're not mad for sex, marry an older type of man who thinks Viagra is a waterfall. *(Emma Bunton)*

Never tell your wife she's lousy in bed. She'll go out and get a second opinion. *(Rodney Dangerfield)*

Marry in haste, repent in Reno. *(Hedda Hopper)*

When you marry, Sally, grab a chump. Tap his forehead first,
and if it rings solid don't hesitate. All the unhappy marriages
come from the husbands having brains. *(P.G. Wodehouse)*

Never marry a man you wouldn't want to be divorced from.
(Nora Ephron)

Never trust a husband too far – or a bachelor too near.
(Helen Rowland)

The best way to remember your wife's birthday is to
forget it once. *(Desi Arnaz)*

If you're looking for monogamy you'd better marry a swan.
(Nora Ephron)

Keep your eyes wide open before marriage,
and half shut afterwards. *(Benjamin Franklin)*

People who wish to get married should actually have met before
deciding to do so. *(William Whitelaw)*

If the coffee is lousy, don't say so. Just throw it on the floor.
*(Raymond Chandler's advice for husbands on how to have a
happy marriage)*

Never feel remorse for what you have thought about your
wife, for she has thought much worse things about you.
(Jean Rostand)

Better to have loved and lost than to have married her, had a
shitload of children and been forced to attend all those
PT meetings. *(Joseph Glynn)*

When you go forth to find a wife, leave your eyes at home, but take both ears with you. *(Sean Gaffney)*

Take an interest in your wife's hobbies. Hire a private detective. *(Sean Kilroy)*

Don't have any children. It makes divorce so much more complicated. *(Albert Einstein)*

A word of advice to those of you about to marry. Don't. *(Rodney Dangerfield)*

Thou Shalt Not Commit Adultery

When the cat's away, it's probably mating. *(Jilly Cooper)*

I have frequently been faithful to my wife. *(Gerald Kennedy)*

50% of the male motivation to stray can be found in a man's
genes. The other 50% can be ound in a woman's jeans.
(Derek McGovern)

The first thrill of adultery is entering the house. Everything has
been paid for my the other man. *(John Updike)*

The one charm of marriage is that it makes a life of deception
absolutely necessary for both parties. *(Oscar Wilde)*

The woman who is adulterous in her own home must
always remember one thing. Put the toilet seat down.
(William Cole)

A man can have two, maybe three love affairs while he's married.
But three is the absolute maximum. After that you're cheating.
(Yves Montand)

I know many married men. I even know a few happily married
ones. But I don't know one who wouldn't fall down the first
open coal-hole running after the first pretty girl who gave
him a wink. *(George Jean Nathan)*

My split from Phyllis George was the first of my four marriages
where the cause of the break-up wasn't infidelity ... but that's
only because I never got caught. *(Robert Evans)*

A survey was done on the nocturnal habits of men. The results showed that 5% got up to drink a glass of water, 10% got up to go to the bathroom, and 85% got up to go home. *(Joe Uris)*

Once a woman has forgiven her man, she must not re-heat his sins for breakfast. *(Marlene Dietrich)*

I'm not telling anybody, 'If you're not happy, go out and screw around because your wife will become a dynamo for you', but I got to be honest with you, that's what happened to me. *(Garth Brooks)*

I have good-looking kids. Thank goodness my wife cheats on me. *(Rodney Dangerfield)*

Men are now entitled to paternity leave. This is when they're allowed out of the office to see if they can find out who the father is. *(Guy Browning)*

We had a perfect marriage until my wife found out the Book of the Month Club didn't hold meetings. *(Bob Monkhouse)*

The French would sooner forgive an extra-marital affair than a bad haircut. *(Helena Powell)*

80% of married men cheat in America. The rest cheat in Europe. *(Jackie Mason)*

A husband discovers his wife having sex with another man. 'What are you doing in bed with my wife?' he exclaims. 'You see?' the wife says to her lover, 'I told you he was stupid.' *(Dave Allen)*

Husbands are chiefly good lovers when they're betraying
their wives. *(Marilyn Monroe)*

I discovered my wife in bed with another man. I was crushed
so I said, 'Get off me, you two.' *(Emo Philips)*

A man thought his wife was having an affair with the milkman
but when he went home the first thing he saw was the baker.
In bed with the milkman. *(Dave Allen)*

My boyfriend had no trouble committing. Adultery.
(Wendy Liebman)

According to a new survey, 60% of married women say they
would rather take a shower with Russell Crowe than with
their own husband. Apparently the remaining 40% couldn't
be reached because they were showering with Russell Crowe.
(Conan O'Brien)

When my husband is late for dinner I know he's either having an
affair or lying dead in the street. I always hope it's the street.
(Jessica Tandy)

It's hard to keep your wife in the dark if you're burning the
candle at both ends. *(Mort Sahl)*

I began to get worried about the fact that my wife might be
having an affair when we moved from Dublin to Donegal
and ended up with the same milkman. *(Conal Gallen)*

I knew it was time to stop cheating when I was with my
girlfriend and I found myself fantasizing about my wife.
(Mick Jagger)

I said to my friend, 'I have a clever wife.' He said, 'Mine always finds out too.' *(Milton Berle)*

88% of the women in the world disapproved of Tiger Woods' extra-marital affairs. The other 12% are cocktail waitresses. *(Jay Leno)*

I told my wife I was seeing a psychiatrist. She told me she was seeing a milkman, a bartender and two plumbers. *(Rodney Dangerfield)*

McDougall found a pair of crutches in the attic so he went downstairs and broke his wife's leg. *(Des MacHale)*

I think my wife is on drugs. I came home unexpectedly the other day and the phone rang. When I picked it up, she said, 'Is the dope still there?' *(Gene Fitzpatrick)*

My friend asked me how long I was wearing a corset. I said, 'Since my wife found it in the back of the car!' *(Tommy Makem)*

Many a husband kisses with his eyes wide open. He wants to make sure his wife isn't around to catch him. *(Anthony Quinn)*

I wasn't kissing her. I was whispering in her mouth. *(Chico Marx's excuse to his wife when she saw him kissing another woman)*

I've always found it more dangerous to fool with a man's mistress than his wife. *(Harold Robbins)*

I walked in on my wife and the milkman. The first thing she said was, 'Don't tell the butcher!' *(Rodney Dangerfield)*

When I said I didn't sleep with married men, what I meant was that I didn't sleep with happily married men. *(Britt Ekland)*

Many a wife thinks her husband is the world's greatest lover: she just can't catch him at it. *(Hal Roach)*

Why go out for hamburger when you can have steak at home? *(Paul Newman)*

When I was married I was always going missing. Miss America, Miss Jamaica, Miss Peru... *(George Best)*

There's a woman for every man in this world. And he's damn lucky if his wife doesn't find out about her. *(Jackie Mason)*

Showbiz Marriages

Richard Burton is alleged to have broken up seven marriages during his twelve years in Hollywood. *(Sam Kashner)*

It was ages before I realized what was wrong with my marriage to Debbie Reynolds but then one day it dawned on me. Everything. *(Eddie Fisher)*

Rhonda Fleming worked out a scheme for staying married to her husband: They intended never to be separated for longer than three weeks at a time. In Hollywood things happen more quickly than elsewhere; the seven year itch starts after three weeks apparently. *(Tom Wiseman)*

In Hollywood a marriage is successful if it outlasts milk. *(Rita Rudner)*

My marriage to Joan Fontaine roughly coincided with World War II. Enough said? *(Brian Aherne)*

'Listen, buddy, I only *play* the Terminator: you married one.' *(Arnold Schwarzenneger to Tom Arnold about Roseanne)*

Our marriage works because we both carry clubs of equal sizes. *(Paul Newman)*

A famous actor's wife sued her husband for divorce and named his mirror as co-respondent. *(Stanley Davis)*

Peter Sellers had four wives and eight heart attacks. Two coronaries per wife is about average. *(Peter Cook)*

There are basically two types of exercise in Hollywood
these days: Jogging and helping divorced friends move.
(Robert Wagner)

Movie stars and monogamy go together like cornflakes
and Tabasco. *(Julia Llewellyn Smith)*

In Hollywood the girl throwing the bouquet at a wedding is just
as likely to be the next one to marry as the girl who catches it.
(Geraldine Page)

That son of a bitch is acting even when he takes his pyjamas off.
(Carole Lombard of her husband William Powell)

I'll never forget the night I brought my Oscar home. Tony
took one look at it and I knew my marriage was over.
(Shelley Winters on Tony Franciosa)

There's a group for men in Hollywood called Divorce
Anonymous. It works like this. If a member of the group
starts to feel the urge to divorce, they send over an
accountant to talk him out of it. *(Sean Connery)*

I liked Rex (Harrison) before we got married and after we got
divorced. It was the bit in between that was the problem.
(Elizabeth Harris)

A Hollywood marriage is a great way to spend a weekend.
(Mort Sahl)

Before marriage a girl has to make love to a man to hold him.
After marriage she had to hold him to make love to him.
(Marilyn Monroe)

I knew Elizabeth Taylor when she didn't know where her next
husband was coming from. *(Johnny Carson)*

I had to set my hair on fire to make news.
You only had to get married.
(Telegram from Michael Jackson to Elton John in 1984)

All I ever got from Hollywood was three lousy ex-husbands.
(Ava Gardner)

Marilyn Monroe's marriage to Joe DiMaggio didn't work out
because he found out she wasn't Marilyn Monroe. Her
marriage to Arthur Miller didn't work out because he found
out she was. *(Billy Wilder)*

In Hollywood, if a guy's wife looks like a new woman – she
probably is. *(Dean Martin)*

There wasn't a wet eye in the house.
*(Dan Naughton on the wedding of Michael Jackson and
Lisa-Marie Presley)*

Ben Affleck's ideal woman would be a stripper with a Budweiser
in each hand. *(Gwyneth Paltrow)*

It wasn't so much a shotgun wedding as a flashbulb one.
(Eddie Fisher on being married to Debbie Reynolds)

Tennis is very big in Hollywood. It's the only chance an actress
gets to wear white. *(Jerry Colonna)*

Hollywood men are either married, going through a divorce, or
want to do your hair. *(Doris Day)*

A Hollywood aristocrat is someone who can trace his ancestry all the way back to his father. *(Jay Leno)*

A Hollywood marriage is one where both parties agree to be faithful until after the honeymoon. *(David McCallum)*

The reason Mickey Rooney divorced seven times was because his wives didn't understand him. *(Jan Chamberlain)*

The Delights of Conversation

In the first year of marriage he talks and she listens. In the second year she talks and he listens. The third year, they both talk and the neighbours listen. *(Donald McGill)*

My wife has an impediment in her speech. Every now and then she stops to take a breath. *(Kevin Goldstein-Jackson)*

My mother-in-law speaks through her nose. She has to – her mouth is worn out. *(Des MacHale)*

My husband says, 'Roseanne, don't you think we ought to talk about our sexual problems?' Like I'm going to turn off 'Wheel of Fortune' for that? *(Roseanne)*

Love means never having to say you're sorry. Marriage means having to say everything twice. *(Estelle Getty)*

Do I speak to my wife during sex? Of Course – if there's a phone handy. *(Henny Youngman)*

My wife said I never listen to her. At least that's what I *think* she said. *(Milton Berle)*

I told my friend I was going to divorce my wife because she hasn't spoken to me in six months. He said, 'Think it over. Wives like that are hard to get.' *(Don Rickles)*

You must come to our house next time. Absolute peace. Neither of us ever says a word to each other. That's the secret of a successful union. *(Alan Ayckbourn)*

I don't mind my wife having the last word. In fact I'm delighted when she reaches it. *(Walter Matthau)*

'One more word,' she said, 'and I'll go back to my mother.'
He said, 'Taxi!' *(Ernie Kovacs)*

I'm hoarse listening to my wife complaining. *(Brendan Behan)*

My son's first film role was that of a man who was married for thirty years. I told him to stick at it and next time he might get a speaking part. *(Henry Fonda)*

Poor old Lord Montlake, who had only two topics of conversation – his gout and his wife. I could never make out which of the two he was talking about. *(Oscar Wilde)*

Male Chauvinists

My notion of a wife at forty is that a man should be
   able to change her, like a banknote, for two twenties.
   (Douglas Jerrold)

A considerate husband is one who remembers to oil the
   lawnmower for his wife before he goes out to play golf.
   (Les Dawson)

When men discover a girl hasn't been with anyone else they
   react in one of three ways. They either want to take you
   home to meet their mother before marrying you, plant their
   flag where no one else has been or pat you on the head like a
   little sister. *(Lulu)*

When two people marry they become in the eyes of the
   law one person – and that one person is the husband.
   (Shana Alexander)

Men only call themselves feminists in the hope of getting a more
   intelligent fuck. *(Kathy Lette)*

In a two-car family, the wife always has the smaller car.
   (Ruth Rendell)

My father did the dishes on Christmas Day so mum could put
   her feet up. This was his entire contribution to the domestic
   set-up. *(Rhona Cameron)*

I never mistreated a girl in my life – except for the ones I
   married. You have to pay for that privilege. *(James Caan)*

If you have a female child, set her to sewing and not reading. Teach her to be useful in the house – to make bread, clean chickens, sift, cook, launder and spin, put new feet into socks and so on. Then when you marry her off she won't look like an ignoramus. *(Paolo de Certaldo)*

A bone for my dog, a stick for my wife. *(Galician proverb)*

Life's a bitch, and then you marry one. *(Chubby Brown)*

Marriage is a custom brought about by women who then proceed to live off men and destroy them, completely enveloping them in a destructive cocoon and eating away at them like a poisonous fungus on a tree. *(Richard Harris)*

A wife should be at the sink or in the bed. *(Dylan Thomas)*

Feminism encourages women to leave their husbands, kill their children, practice witchcraft, destroy capitalism and become lesbians. *(Rev. Pat Robertson at a Republican convention in 1992)*

He who knocks his wife about thoroughly will be forgiven a hundred sins. *(Estonian proverb)*

Every husband may beat his wife when she disobeys his commands or when she curses or contradicts him, provided he does it moderately and not to the extent of causing her death. *(Philippe de Beaumanoir)*

These days I wouldn't be caught dead with a woman old enough to be my wife. *(Tony Curtis)*

There are no father-in-law jokes. *(Bernice Sandler)*

Marriage is very difficult. Very few of us are fortunate enough to marry multi-millionaire girls with 39-inch busts who have undergone frontal lobotomies. *(Tony Curtis)*

If a woman and her adulterer are killed by her husband or fiancé, he shall pay no fine for the homicide. *(Spanish law of 1240)*.

Trouble and Strife

Your marriage is in trouble if your wife says, 'You're only
interested in one thing'...and you can't remember what it is.
(Milton Berle)

When did I first become aware of problems within our marriage?
I suppose it was around the time he started bonking
the au pair. *(Jill Saunders)*

You know your marriage is in trouble when new jars have suddenly
appeared in the kitchen labeled 'Anthrax' and 'Cyanide'.
(Geoff Tibballs)

Some people claim that marriage interferes with romance. It's
true. Anytime you're trying to have some romance,
your wife interferes. *(Groucho Marx)*

The main problem in marriage is when the couple is
incompatible. This can be alleviated somewhat if the husband
has enough income and the wife is pattable. *(Sid Caesar)*

Some stuff about being married bothers me. Like having a husband.
(Roseanne Barr)

There are two kinds of people in the world. The first kind always
wants the television on the second kind always wants it off.
Unfortunately they usually happen to be married to one another.
(Frank Sinatra)

My wife and I are inseparable. Sometimes it takes four people to
pull us apart. *(Milton Berle)*

Do you think we should have got an army without conscription
if domestic life had been as happy as people say it is?
(George Bernard Shaw)

If it has tyres or testicles you're going to have problems with it.
(Linda Furney)

It's very difficult being married to Joan of Arc.
(Roger Vadim on Jane Fonda)

The main problem with marriage is that it involves two kinds of
people who can never get on: men and women. *(Sid Caesar)*

If a husband has troubles he should tell his wife. And if he hasn't
he should tell the world how he does it. *(Red Buttons)*

We sleep in separate rooms, we have dinner apart, we take
separate vacations. We're doing everything we can to keep
our marriage together. *(Rodney Dangerfield)*

My husband said he needed more space so I locked him outside.
(Roseanne)

Any man who's married can appreciate why we've named our
hurricanes after women. *(Art Buchwald)*

Our marriage is based on trust and understanding. She doesn't
trust me and I don't understand her. *(Bob Monkhouse)*

If you marry the right woman there's nothing like it and if you
marry the wrong woman there's nothing like it. *(Sid Caesar)*

From 'I Do' to 'Adieu'

Divorce comes from the Latin word 'divorceum', which
   means 'Having your genitals torn out through your wallet'.
   (Robin Williams)

My wife got the house, the car and the bank balance. And
   if I marry again and have children she gets them too.
   (Woody Allen)

The happiest time of anyone's life is just after the first divorce.
   (Kenneth Galbraith)

What a holler would ensure if people had to pay the minister as
   much to marry them as they have to pay a lawyer to get them
   a divorce. *(Claire Trevor)*

My wife and I had an amicable divorce. She lets me see my
   stuff at weekends. Last Sunday I took my sweaters to
   Disneyland. *(Craig Shoemaker)*

It was an ideal divorce: she got the children and he got the maid.
   (Joan Rivers)

Why did I divorce? Because my husband was an asshole.
   Any more questions? *(Roseanne)*

The two most important causes of divorce? Men and women.
   (Sid Caesar)

Dahling, this time I married a lawyer so he could handle the
   divorce. *(Zsa Zsa Gabor)*

Marriage is grand. Divorce is twenty grand. *(Jackie Mason)*

Why does divorce cost so much? Because it's worth it.
(Johnny Carson)

One marriage in four ends in divorce. The other three fight it
out to the bitter end. *(Lucille Ball)*

Did you hear about the new 'divorced' Barbie Doll? It comes
with all of Ken's stuff. *(Sid Caesar)*

Getting divorced because you don't love somebody is as silly as
getting married because you do. *(Zsa Zsa Gabor)*

Every divorce ends with a fight over who gets the side table.
(Claire Bloom)

Divorce happens when you haven't been home for 18 years.
(Lee Trevino)

Heather Mills got a 24 million divorce settlement. Wow,
she really landed on her foot. *(John Inverdale)*

They wanted to allow divorced women to compete in the
Miss America pageant. I don't think that's a good idea. Do
you really want to hear, 'My dreams for the future include
world peace, and that my ex-husband gets killed by a bus'?
(Jay Leno)

When I was a teenager I asked my mother, 'Mom,
are you and Dad getting a divorce?' She
said 'No, I'm just drying your father's clothes.'
But he was in them at the time. *(Robert Murray)*

When you start to feel married, that's when you should divorce.
(Mick Jagger)

For a while my wife and I pondered whether to take a vacation
or get a divorce. We decided that a trip to Bermuda is over
in two weeks but a divorce is something you always have.
(Woody Allen)

When my parents got divorced there was a custody fight over me
but no one showed up. *(Rodney Dangerfield)*

Dividing stuff up is one of the most parts of divorce as suddenly
you and your ex discover that both of you cannot live
without the tea towels of the Isle of Wight or the toaster that
doesn't really work. *(David Quantick)*

I've given my memoirs far more thought than any of my
marriages. You can't divorce a book. *(Gloria Swanson)*

I knew a guy who had a heart attack so he got a pacemaker. His
wife divorced him because she said it interfered with the TV.
(Walter Matthau)

Just because divorce was beyond your parents doesn't mean
that it's beyond you. It won't be easy. You'll have to dig deep
inside your heart for inspiration. *(Keith Barret)*

The best grounds for divorce are wherever you're standing.
(Johnny Lyons)

It's hard to talk to men you've divorced because they take things
the wrong way. You say, 'Nice day, don't you think? And they
go, 'I don't want to make a commitment.' *(Elayne Boosler)*

I've just got rid of ten pounds of ugly fat – I divorced the wife.
(Roy Brown)

Divorce has become so common now, my wife and myself are staying together just to be different. *(Leopold Fechtner)*

My husband and I had a very messy divorce because there was a baby involved, him. And I didn't want custody.
(Wendy Liebman)

When I got divorced I went through the various stages of grieving – anger, denial, dancing around with my settlement cheque...
(Maura Kennedy)

Judging by the divorce rate, a lot of people who say 'I do', don't.
(Hal Roach)

All the Money

The judge said 'All the money'. But then they shortened it to 'Alimony.' *(Robin Williams)*

Alimony is always having to say you're sorry. *(Philip Sinborg)*

Marriage is only for a little while; it's alimony that lasts forever. *(Quentin Crisp)*

Henry VIII didn't get divorced; he just had his wives' heads chopped off when he got tired of them. That's a good way to get rid of a woman. No alimony. *(Ted Turner)*

You never realise how short a month is until you pay alimony. *(John Barrymore)*

I'm trying to find my ex-wife a suitable new husband so I don't have to pay her alimony anymore. But, Ivan the Terrible is dead, isn't he? *(Peter O'Toole)*

The wages of sin is alimony. *(Carolyn Wells)*

I sometimes wonder if the fucking you get is worth the fucking you got. *(Humphrey Bogart)*

Instead of getting married again I'm going to find a woman I don't like and just give her my house. *(Rod Stewart)*

An actress is a woman with no ability who spends most of her time sitting around the place waiting to go on alimony. *(Jackie Stallone)*

Not Making the Same Mistake Once

A bachelor is a guy who never made the same mistake once. *(Phyllis Diller)*

If there's a realistic deterrent to marriage it's the fact that you can't afford divorce. *(Jack Nicholson)*

I'm not exactly scared of marriage. It's just that, looking around, it never works. *(Julie Christie)*

I once heard of a marriage that broke up because he wanted to squeeze the toothpaste from the top of the tube and his wife from the bottom. That put me off a bit. *(Cliff Richard)*

He marries best who puts it off until it's too late. *(H.L. Mencken)*

By persistently remaining single a man converts himself into a permanent public temptation. *(Oscar Wilde)*

I have never married because there was no need. I have three pets at home that serve the same purpose as a husband; a dog that growls every morning, a parrot that swears all afternoon and a cat that comes home late at night. *(Marie Corelli)*

I'm afraid of commitment. I'd get married if they changed the wedding vow to 'Do I?' *(Al Lubel)*

The closest I've come to tying the knot was during a bizarre bondage session with an incredibly attractive but completely psychotic Swiss girl called Lucia in an Amsterdam hotel. *(Olaf Tyaransen)*

I can marry anyone I please. The trouble is, I haven't pleased anyone yet. *(Wendy Miller)*

There's only one thing in the world better than a good wife... no wife. *(Sean Gaffney)*

I'm single by choice. Not my own one. *(Rosie Willis)*

Why get married and make one person miserable when I can stay single and do the same for thousands? *(Carrie Snow)*

Some men get what they deserve. Others remain bachelors. *(Ernest Forbes)*

Bachelors believe in the happiness of pursuit. *(Wyn Jenkins)*

I will never marry again never. Being married means making excuses and I'm not a good liar. To lie you have to have a good memory and I can't remember anything I've done for years. *(Richard Harris)*

I'm married to not being married. *(Al Pacino)*

I have so little regard for myself that I didn't even invite myself to my own wedding. *(Colin Farrell)*

Why buy a cow when you can get free milk? *(Elvis Presley)*

Being an old maid is like death by drowning: a delightful sensation after you cease to struggle. *(Edna Ferber)*

Bachelors should be heavily taxed – it's not fair that some men should be happier than others. *(Oscar Wilde)*

If there's one thing that puts me off marriage it's women.
  (Bill Naughton)

I've had a lot of very good friends. I've always liked them too
  much to marry them. *(Lillian Gish)*

I never married because it would have meant giving up my
  favourite hobby. Men. *(Mae West)*

A bachelor is a man who comes to work from a different
  direction every morning. *(George Coote)*

I would not marry God.
  (Maxine Elliott after her engagement was rumoured)

A bachelor never gets over the idea that he's a thing of beauty
  and a boy forever. *(Helen Rowland)*

I think, therefore I'm single. *(Graffiti)*

I'm giving up marriage for Lent. *(Brian Behan)*

As far as I know, a single man has never vacuumed behind a couch.
  (Rita Rudner)

I have no intention of getting married. To me, marriage
  essentially is a contract and there are so many
  loopholes in it that Wilbur Mills and the entire
  Ways and Means Committee couldn't figure it out.
  (Warren Beatty – before he got married)

Once More with Feeling

I'm going to marry again because I'm more mature now. And I need some kitchen stuff. *(Wendy Liebman)*

Liz Taylor and Richard Burton split up but they didn't like it and re-married. But they didn't like that either so they split up again. This could have gone on until they both died. *(Jo Brand)*

My wife and I got re-married. The divorce didn't work out. *(Henny Youngman)*

I think every woman is entitled to a middle husband she can forget. *(Adele Rogers St.John)*

Would I consider re-marriage? Yes, if I found a man who had $15 million who would sign over half of it to me before becoming my husband and guarantee he'd be dead within a year. *(Bette Davis)*

Some people are obsessed with the whole idea of marriage. A woman named Adrienne Cuyot from France was engaged 652 times and married 53 times over a period of 23 years. *(Richard Wilson)*

People blame me for divorcing my three husbands. They forget that they had twenty wives between them. *(Ava Gardner)*

Some women have affairs but unfortunately I marry my men. It's funny that a woman can have 25 affairs and nobody says anything but if she has 4 husbands she's terrible. I guess I'm just a homebody. *(Hedy Lamarr)*

After divorcing his first wife, Mark Thatcher has married again. And who's the lucky lady? Well the first wife, obviously. *(Clive Anderson)*

Ike Turner is single again. His thirteenth wife has left him. She came home unexpectedly and caught him punching out another woman. *(Jay Leno)*

Four must be my unlucky number. I married my fourth husband in 1964 and about four weeks was all I could stand with the fella. *(Ethel Merman)*

Many a man owes his success to his first wife and his second wife to his success. *(Jim Backus)*

Lenny (Henry) and myself renewed our wedding vows in Las Vegas. I laughed so much I wet my knickers. It makes a mockery of everything you think about marriage. Plastic flowers, Velcro-fastened dresses and a preacher who had to look at a prompt sheet to remember your name. *(Dawn French)*

Zsa Zsa Gabor got married as a one-off but it was so successful she turned it into a series. *(Bob Hope)*

I shall marry in haste and repeat at leisure. *(James Branch Cabell)*

Bigamy proves that two rites make a wrong. *(Phil Kelly)*

I've only been married three times and had three or four lovers. On today's market that's practically a virgin. *(Shelley Winters)*

People keep asking me if I'll marry again. Why would I want to go from one car crash to another? *(Stephanie Beacham)*

My thirteenth wife cried and the judge wiped her tears with my chequebook. *(Tommy Manville)*

My grandfather had been married twice, a state which in Wales is looked upon rather like leprosy. *(Ray Milland)*

I was once asked for my opinion of monogamy. I replied that I believed it made the best coffee tables. *(Lee Van Cleef)*

I can't for the life of me understand why people keep insisting marriage is doomed. All five of mine worked out. *(Peter de Vries)*

Daffynitions

A wife is a woman who can look in a drawer and find a pair of her husband's socks that aren't there. *(Dan Bennett)*

A husband is a man who uses both hands to drive the car. *(Leopold Fechtner)*

A newlywed is a guy who tells his wife when he gets a pay raise. *(Leonard Levinson)*

A widow may be defined as a woman who knows where her husband is every night. *(Dave Allen)*

A liberated woman is one who has sex before marriage and a job after it. *(Gloria Steinem)*

A divorcee is a woman who got married so she didn't have to work but now works so she doesn't have to get married. *(Anna Magnani)*

Love is the quest, marriage the conquest and divorce the inquest. *(Helen Rowland)*

Morality consists of suspecting people of not being married. *(George Bernard Shaw)*

Divorce is a system whereby two people make a mistake and one of them goes on paying for it. *(Len Deighton)*

Bigamy is having one husband too many. Monogamy is the same. *(Erica Jong)*

Alimony is the ransom the happy pay to the devil.
(Ambrose Bierce)

A bigamist is a man who has the bad taste to do what
conscience and the police keep the rest of us from doing.
(Finlay Peter Dunne)

A perfectionist is a man who, if he was married to Marilyn
Monroe, would expect her to cook. *(Dan Bennett)*

Who Rules the Roost?

Isn't marriage wonderful? To be able to sit in your own home, relax, drink beer all night and watch your wife's favourite programmes. *(Leopold Fechtner)*

Marriage by its nature is less fair to women. Adam didn't cook, and he never spent enough time with Cain and Abel. *(Bette Davis)*

It was time to tell my wife who was the boss so I thought it out very carefully. I waited until I was feeling in the right frame of mind, took a stiff drink, drew myself up to my full height and said to her, 'Honey, you're the boss.' *(Michael Harkness)*

I wear the pants in our house but I also wash and iron them. *(Denis Thatcher)*

Only two things are necessary to keep one's wife happy. First, let her think she's having her way. Second, let her have it. *(Lyndon B. Johnson)*

I was born Mary Patterson but then I got married and took my husband's name. So now I'm Neil Patterson. *(A Bit of Fry and Laurie)*

I believe in marriage but there ain't goin' to be no equality. If a woman wants to be equal with me, let her get her own Rolls-Royce, her own house and her own million dollars. *(Muhammad Ali)*

We have a 50-50 marriage. She cooks and I eat. *(Les Dawson)*

Any woman who thinks marriage is a 50/50 proposition either doesn't understand men or percentages. *(Florynce Kennedy)*

A wise woman will always let her husband have her way. *(Richard Brinsley Sheridan)*

Sleeping with the Enemy

If you think women are the weaker sex, try pulling the duvet over to your side. *(Paul Gleeson)*

Research has shown that men usually sleep on the right side of the bed. Even in their sleep they happen to be right. *(Rita Rudner)*

Laugh and the world laughs with you. Quarrel with your wife and you sleep alone. *(George Coote)*

I was reading an article that was discussing a rare medical condition in which people actually have sex while they're asleep. Now correct me if I'm wrong but isn't that called marriage? *(David Letterman)*

My wife and I have an agreement that we never go to sleep angry with one another. We've been awake now for six months. *(Brendan Grace)*

Marriage was not a guy's idea. A woman came up with it and the guy said, 'Lemme get this straight. I never sleep with anyone else ever again and if things don't work out you get to keep all my stuff. Great!' *(Bobby Slayton)*

If your husband has difficulty getting to sleep, the words 'We need to talk about our relationship' should help. *(Rita Rudner)*

Gilbert Roland was a wonderful husband in one room of the house. *(Constance Bennett)*

I was in confession. I said to the priest, 'Father, is it a sin to sleep with your boyfriend?' He said, 'No, my child, it's only a sin if you stay awake.' *(Peg Sanders)*

An American wife who can prove her husband snores can get a divorce any time she likes. In Reno they understand. *(Anthony Cotterel)*

If you're married to someone, you don't have enough room in the bed and you might have to face bad breath in the morning. That's enough to put me off. *(Andy Warhol)*

At some point in a marriage – even the strongest marriage – one person or the other is going to get restless and have at least a twinge of a thought about sleeping with someone else. For some people this desire occurs about six times a minute. For others it occurs around age forty. The thing to keep in mind is that nobody gets into bed with the same person every night for a period of years and listens to them passing wind without as least imagining a more alluring alternative. *(Wendy Dennis)*

You know you're married when you sleep all night in the wet spot. And it's comprised of spilled chocolate milk. *(Buzz Nutley)*

Odious Comparisons

Being married to Lana Turner was like sitting in a room with a beautiful vase. *(Artie Shaw)*

A woman who takes her husband about with her everywhere is like a cat that goes on playing with a mouse long after she's killed it. *(H.H. Munro)*

Paying alimony is like feeding hay to a dead horse. *(Groucho Marx)*

Divorce is the psychological equivalent of a triple coronary bypass. *(Mary Kay Blakely)*

My wife is as cold as the hairs on a polar bear's bum. *(Les Dawson)*

My marriage to Bill Arnold was like a close-up of tooth decay. *(Roseanne)*

Being married to Sean Connery was like being married to a golf course. *(Diane Cilento)*

The marriage between Richard Burton and Liz Taylor was about as tranquil as a bad gear change in a ten-foot lorry. *(Donald Zec)*

Being married to Greg Allman was like going to Disneyland on acid. You know you had a good time but can't remember what you did. *(Cher)*

A bit like going on vacation with your ex-wife. *(Andrea Glynn on the reunion of Simon & Garfunkel)*

The majority of husbands remind me of an orangutan trying to play the violin. *(Balzac)*

Marriage is like throwing yourself in the river when you only want a drink. *(David Jason)*

Love and marriage go together like angel cake and anthrax. *(Julie Birchill)*

Giving birth is like taking your lower lip and forcing it over your head. *(Carol Burnett)*

Dreadful flowers bought at a garage were a perfect metaphor for my wedding to Chris Evans: last minute, cheap and dead within hours. *(Carol McGiffin)*

The Vietnam war finally ended in an agreement neither side ever intended to honour. It was like one of Zsa Zsa Gabor's weddings. *(Bob Hope)*

Getting married is like burning your house down to get a piece of toast. *(Sean Kilroy)*

Women are like elephants. I like to look at them but I wouldn't want to own one. *(W.C. Fields)*

It's not easy being in a group. It's like marriage without sex. *(Sting)*

George Bush reminds every woman of her first husband. *(Jane O'Reilly)*

My wife has a face like a million dollars – all green and wrinkled. *(Noel V. Ginnity)*

Being married was like having a hippopotamus sitting
    on my face. *(Faith Sullivan)*

Marriage is like a tornado. They both begin with a lot of
    blowing and sucking and in the end you lose your house.
    (Conan O'Brien)

My mother-in-law thinks I'm effeminate. Compared to her, I
    probably am. *(Les Dawson)*

The Demon Drink

I doubt if my wife and I will ever get on. She can't stand me
   when I'm drunk and I can't stand her when I'm sober.
   (Fred Metcalf)

90% of ulcers are married ones. They come from mortgages,
   commuter rides, yard work, flooded basements and fighting
   over who leaves the toilet lid up and why she calls the bar to
   see if he left yet. *(Mike Royko)*

Q. What do all men in singles bars have in common?
A. They're married.
   (Sandra Frears)

I met my wife in a bar. What a surprise. I thought she was at
   home minding the kids. *(Henny Youngman)*

Men have two reasons for staying at the pub all night.
   Either they've got no wives to go home to or they have.
   (Kris Kristofferson)

The worst thing Michael Jackson was ever guilty of was
   causing middle-aged drunk people at weddings to try and
   do the moonwalk. *(Billy Connolly)*

I sold my wife to a guy for a bottle of scotch and now I wish I
   had her back because I'm thirsty again. *(Henny Youngman)*

Apparently man can be cured of drugs, drink, gambling, biting
   his nails and picking his nose – but not of marrying.
   (William Faulkner)

'I love you more than anything in the world,' I said. I was holding
a wine bottle in my hand. My wife said, 'That's the drink
talking.' I said, 'No, it was me. But I was talking to the drink.'
(Noel V. Ginnity)

There are all kinds of magazines for brides but I think they
should have a bridesmaids one too, with helpful articles
like 'Should You Get Drunk and Sleep with the Best Man
at the Rehearsal Dinner or Wait Until After the Ceremony?'
(Kelly Maguire)

I met my wife in a New York bar. We had a lot in common.
We were both from California and we were both drunk.
(Tug McGraw)

After our wedding we looked like a new house. She was freshly
painted and I was plastered. *(Leopold Fechtner)*

The bottle is like a second wife to Richard Burton – and who
wants to break up a happy marriage? *(Kenneth Tynan)*

Whiskey is a drink that makes you see double and feel single.
(Brendan Grace)

My wife drove me to drink and I didn't have the courtesy to
thank her. *(W.C. Fields)*

Anniversaries

I've just marked my tenth anniversary on the calendar...by throwing darts at it. *(Phyllis Diller)*

I have a friend whose husband married her on February 29th so he could only forget their anniversary every four years. *(Ann Davis)*

My wife and I have just celebrated our 30th wedding anniversary. If I'd killed her the first time I thought about it I'd have been out of prison by now. *(Frank Carson)*

I asked my wife, 'Where do you want to go for our anniversary?' She said, 'Somewhere I've never been.' I said, 'How about the kitchen?' *(Henny Youngman)*

Wedding anniversaries are a bit like toilets. Men tend to miss them. *(Jo Brand)*

My parents have just passed their silver and gold anniversaries. The next one is rust. *(Rita Rudner)*

My parents celebrated their 43rd wedding anniversary. My mother doesn't like to hear me talking about divorce. 'You gotta learn how to work these things out,' she says. 'Your father and I had a shoot-out. He took one in the arm. He was wrong so I shot him. You move on.' *(Wanda Sykes)*

Next to privacy, the rarest thing in Hollywood is a wedding anniversary. *(Gene Fowler)*

Always The Bride, Never the Bridesmaid

Your heart knows when you meet the right man.
(Liz Taylor at her wedding to Nicky Hilton in 1950)

For me this is the beginning of a happy end. *(Taylor after she divorced Hilton to marry Michael Wilding two years later).*

This marriage will last forever. For me it will be third time lucky. *(Taylor after divorcing Wilding to marry Mike Todd in 1957).*

I have never been happier in my life. We will be on our honeymoon for thirty or forty years. *(Taylor at her wedding to Eddie Fisher two years later, Todd having been killed in a plane crash).*

I'm so happy you can't believe it. *(Taylor after divorcing Fisher to marry Richard Burton in 1964).*

There will be no more marriages or divorces. We're stuck like chicken feathers to tar. *(Taylor after re-marrying Burton in 1975. They'd divorced in 1974)*

I want to spend the rest of my life with him. I want to be buried with him *(Taylor on John Warner in 1976 after her second marriage to Burton broke down).*

With God's blessing this is it, forever. *(Taylor on her eighth husband Larry Fortensky in 1991. It wasn't)*

Schadenfreude

The best thing about marriage is the security and reassurance it offers. However bad things get in life, it is deeply reassuring to know that there is someone worse off than yourself. *(Guy Browning)*

I love being married. It's great to find that one special person you want to annoy for the rest of your life. *(Rita Rudner)*

I bequeathe all my property to my wife on the condition that she remarry immediately. Then there will be at least one man to regret my death. *(Heinrich Heine)*

I should, on many a good day, have blown my brains out but for the recollection that it would have given pleasure to my mother-in-law. *(Lord Byron)*

I don't think my wife likes me very much. When I had a heart attack she *wrote* for an ambulance. *(Frank Carson)*

My wife doesn't care what I do when I'm away from home as long as I don't have a good time. *(Lee Trevino)*

I know my wife would divorce me if she could find some way of doing it that would make me miserable. *(Milton Berle)*

The best way to get revenge on a man you hate is to marry him. *(Ava Gardner)*

The occasional lacing of my husband's dinner with cat food has done wonders for my spirit. *(Lana Tate)*

Not all women give most of their waking thoughts to the problem of pleasing men. Some are married. *(Emma Lee)*

Licence to Thrill

I'm the only man who has a marriage licence saying To Whom It
May Concern. *(Mickey Rooney)*

Zsa Zsa Gabor has been married so often they don't issue her
with a new marriage licence anymore. They just punch the
old one. *(Johnny Carson)*

Two dollars will buy all the happiness or all the misery in the
world. At least that *used* to be the price of a marriage licence.
(Eddie Cantor)

Marriage is like a car. It starts with a licence and ends with a
wreck. *(Fred Allen)*

Thelma Todd; 'From the time he got our marriage license I've
led a dog's life.'
Groucho Marx: 'Are you sure he didn't get a dog's licence?'
(Monkey Business)

My wife threatened to divorce me so many times, in the
end she just left our marriage license with the solicitor.
(Jimmy White)

Our marriage licence turned out to be a learner's permit.
(Joan Rivers)

I was married once, in San Francisco. I haven't seen her for
many years. The great earthquake of 1906 destroyed the
marriage licence. Which just goes to prove that earthquakes
aren't all bad. *(W.C. Fields)*

Desperate Stratagems

I asked the doctor if he had any sleeping pills for the wife. He gave me a hundred – but she still woke up. *(Roy Brown)*

If I ever marry and have a girl-child I'll drown her like the Chinese. *(John Fante)*

I've often wanted to drown my troubles but I can't get my wife to go swimming. *(Bob Monkhouse)*

One year I bought the wife a fireside chair. It cost me a lot of money. That's why I was annoyed that it fused when I plugged it in. *(Les Dawson)*

There are only about 20 murders a year in London and not all are serious – some are just husbands killing their wives. *(Commander G.H. Hatherill of Scotland Yard in 1954)*

I do a lot of reading on serial killers. Mostly 'How To' books. *(Roseanne)*

My wife and myself hold hands when we're out walking. We're afraid to let go in case we start beating each other up. *(Brendan O'Carroll)*

A man will kill his wife and then kill himself. A woman kills her husband, then does her nails. *(Thomas Lynch)*

Killing your wife is a natural thing that could happen to the best of us. *(Brendan Behan)*

Wedded Bliss

For twenty years my wife and I were deliriously happy.
Then we met. *(Brian Johnston)*

Mrs. Santa Claus is unhappy because her husband has the names
of all the bad little girls. *(Henny Youngman)*

There is a simple secret for marriages that last. Long ago
I forgave my husband for not being Paul Newman.
(Erma Bombeck)

Happiness is having a loyal, loving, beautiful wife –
in another city. *(Henny Youngman)*

One of the first signs that your wife is unhappy is when she
starts lining the budgie's cage with your wedding pictures.
(Roy Brown)

I never knew what real happiness was until I got married but by
then it was too late. *(Max Kaufman)*

Happiness is having your girlfriend's lipstick the same colour as
your wife's. *(Phil Hartman)*

I have a very happy relationship with my wife. I try to see her as
often as I can. *(Brendan Grace)*

The only thing that keeps me from being happily married is
my husband. *(Andrea Douglas)*

I'm very happily divorced. *(Bette Davis)*

The most happy marriage I can picture or imagine to myself would be the union of a deaf man to a blind woman. *(Samuel Taylor Coleridge)*

In Hollywood all marriages are happy. It's trying to live together afterwards that's the problem. *(Shelley Winters)*

No matter how happily a woman may be married, it always pleases her to discover that there's a nice man who wishes she weren't. *(H.L. Mencken)*

Conundrums

Do married people live longer or does it just seem that way?
  (Don Rickles)

If brides wear white to symbolize chastity on the wedding day,
  why do grooms wear black? *(Jack Cruise)*

Why does a woman work 10 years to change a man's habits
  and then complain that he's not the man she married?
  (Barbra Streisand)

If there were no husbands, who would look after our mistresses?
  (George Moore)

They say marriage is an institution but who the hell wants to live
  in an institution? *(Bette Davis)*

There's a curious statistic I came across recently. The average
  married couple converse for twenty minutes every week.
  What do they find to talk about? *(Dave Allen)*

I don't know why Marilyn Monroe married Joe DiMaggio. Why
  marry a ball-player when you can have the whole team?
  (Mae West)

May-December Marriages

It was a May-December romance. She wanted to get married in May and he decided to call it off in December. *(Mort Sahl)*

When Liz Taylor married Larry Fortensky, he was younger than her first wedding dress. *(A.A. Gill)*

Did you hear about the Alabama man who died and left all his money to his widow? She can't touch it till she's 14. *(Dan Fenwick)*

Congratulations are in order for Woody Allen. He and Soon Yi have a brand new baby daughter. It's all part of Woody's plan to grow his own wives. *(David Letterman)*

Joan Collins unfortunately can't be with us tonight. She's busy attending the birth of her next husband. *(John Parrott)*

An old man marrying a young girl is like buying a book for someone else to read. *(H.W. Thompson)*

These days men are walking down the aisle with foetuses in veils. *(Kathy Lette)*

Gifts

Bud Abbott: 'Have you decided what you're giving the bride and groom?'
Lou Costello: 'Yes, about six months.'

I prefer going to funerals than weddings. You don't have to bring a gift. *(Jack Cruise)*

Women are funny. My wife gave me two neckties last Christmas. On Christmas morning I put one of them on, went downstairs, showed it to her, and the first thing she said was, 'What was wrong with the other one?' *(Dave Allen)*

Always make a big to-do about anything your husband gives you. Wear it to bed unless it's a toaster. *(Helen Curley Brown)*

My attitude to sex is simple. Get it over with quickly and then get a gift. *(Joan Rivers)*

Why we stayed together, squabbling constantly, during those first twelve months neither of us can now understand. It probably had something to do with the shame we would have felt at throwing in the marital towel – not to mention having to give back the presents. *(Barry Norman on his first year of marriage)*

There's one absolute rule when it comes to buying a wedding gift. Stay away from food mixers. *(Stanley Baxter)*

Modern Times

Women who remember their fist kiss now have daughters who can't remember their first husbands. *(Henny Youngman)*

These days it's harder to get out of a mortgage than a marriage. *(Germaine Greer)*

Modern drugs are wonderful. They enable a wife with pneumonia to nurse her husband through 'flu. *(Jilly Cooper)*

I love Ireland but they're a tad behind the times. They just voted divorce in. We're about to colonise Mars and they've just voted divorce in. Wow. Hang on for another 2000 years and you might get the *Playboy* channel. *(Denis Leary)*

There's so much permissiveness in the world today, the only way to stop having sex is to get married. *(Brigitte Bardot)*

Brides today are wearing their dresses shorter. And more often. *(Milton Berle)*

The only pre-marital thing girls don't do nowadays is cook. *(Omar Sharif)*

In my day, men were content with ten commandments and one wife. Now the situation is reversed. *(Saki)*

Counselling

My counsellor told my wife we should enjoy sex every night. Now we'll never see each other. *(Chevy Chase)*

A man took his wife along to a marriage counsellor. The counsellor asked him to explain the problem. The man said, 'What's 'er name here claims I don't pay her enough attention.' *(Fred Metcalf)*

Whenever a husband and wife begin to discuss their marriage they're giving evidence at an inquest. *(Elbert Hubbard)*

My counsellor told me my wife just wanted me to say those three little words every woman wants to hear: 'You are right.' *(Steven Summers)*

I've always been unlucky in love. My wife has just run off with the marriage counsellor. *(Paul Murtagh)*

The High Cost of Leaving

Prince Charles is the only member of the Royal Family who ever left Cinderella for the Ugly Duckling. *(Des Hanafin)*

My wife left me. I should have seen it coming. For the past year she called me her Insignificant Other. By the end of the marriage her favourite sexual position was man on top, woman visiting her mother. *(Daniel Liebert)*

Murphy came home from work and got a terrible shock. His wife said she wasn't leaving him. *(Noel V. Ginnity)*

I married a suicide bomber but she went off with somebody else. *(Jeff Green)*

My best friend ran away with my wife. I miss him a lot. *(Joe Cuddy)*

This time of year makes me sad. It was ten years ago today that I lost my wife. I'll never forget that poker game. *(Henny Youngman)*

I take my wife everywhere but she keeps finding her way back. *(Henny Youngman)*

Husband: My wife has just run off with my best friend.
Neighbour: What's his name?
Husband: I don't know. I never met him.
(Don Rickles)

She: 'I'm afraid that after we're married, a beautiful girl will come along and you'll forget all about me.'

He: 'Not at all. I'll write you twice a week.'

(Internet joke)

Wife-Swapping

Wife-swapping is never done in the best circles of society. Wives can rarely, if ever, be traded for anything useful like a set of golf clubs. *(P.J. O'Rourke)*

There's only one thing wrong with wife-swapping. You get another wife. *(Scott Roeben)*

You gotta keep changing. Shirts, old ladies, whatever. *(Neil Young)*

Patrick and Mick were in bed together looking at the ceiling when Patrick said to Mick, 'You know something? This wife-swapping lark isn't really all it's cracked up to be.' *(Michael Harkness)*

Why are there no husband-swapping parties? *(Lily Tomlin)*

The Golden Years

If I reach my fortieth year I'll probably marry an old maid with
  protruding upper teeth left a little exposed by the upper lip.
  (Franz Kafka)

I know an 85-year-old man who married a girl of 18. He wanted
  somebody to answer the Rosary for him. *(Eamon Kelly)*

An 80-year-old man said to his 75-year-old wife, 'I'd like
  to go upstairs and make love.' She said, 'I can't do both.'
  (Noel V. Ginnity)

The older you get, the more you lower your standards in
  husbands. I used to be so picky. It was like, 'Oh, when I get
  married he has to be tall, handsome and rich.' Now I'm down
  to 'Registered Voter.' *(Judy Tenuta)*

My husband's idea of a good night out is a good night in.
  (Maureen Lipman)

He: 'Will you love me when I'm old and grey?'
She: 'I do.'

When you get to sixty, marriage is about spraying each other
  with Ralgex. *(Richard Wilson)*

A man of 90 married a woman of 85. They spent the
  honeymoon trying to get out of the car. *(Hal Roach)*

The Reaper

It's a sad fact that 50% of marriages in America end in divorce.
But hey, the other half end in death. You could be one of the
lucky ones! *(Richard Jeni)*

The only difference between the married and the dead is
that the married get to watch 'Stars in Their Eyes' from
a slouching position whereas the dead are contractually
obliged to be horizontal. *(Ian Pattison)*

The fact that husbands don't live as long as wives can be seen
as nature trying to make up for the inequality of sexism.
Some widows are bereaved but many are simply relieved.
(Rachel Roberts)

The best thing to do after you see your dead husband's body on
the floor is to have a cup of tea. *(Anthony Burgess)*

Everything has its drawbacks, as the man said when his
mother-in-law died and they came down on him for the
funeral expenses. *(Jerome K. Jerome)*

I want to die before my wife. If it's true that when you die your
soul goes for judgment I don't want her up there ahead of me
to tell them things. *(Bill Cosby)*

Mrs. Teasdale: 'My husband is dead.'
Firefly: 'I bet he's just using that as an excuse.'
(Exchange from the movie Duck Soup*).*

I haven't laughed so much since my husband died. *(Joan Rivers)*

Being widowed is God's way of telling you to come off the pill.
    (Victoria Wood)

This chap told me his wife's an angel. He's lucky –
    mine is still alive. *(Bernard Manning)*

I wouldn't trust my husband with a woman for five minutes and
    he's been dead for 25 years. *(Kathleen Behan)*

My mother-in-law said she was going to dance on my grave so I
    told her I intended to be buried at sea. *(Bob Monkhouse)*

Divorce is excruciating. It's like mourning a death, only worse,
    because the damn corpse keeps waking up. *(Erica Jong)*

There were no last words. His wife was with him to the end.
    (Spike Milligan)

Q. How can you tell if your wife is dead?
A. The sex is the same but the dishes are higher in the sink.
    (Brendan Grace)

And Finally...

I brought my wife to Las Vegas with me. You always pack something you don't need. *(Dave Barry)*

I don't like shopping with my wife. She wants to try different things on. I'm different. As soon as she comes out of the dressing room I'm like someone in a bank robbery. 'That's the one – get in the car!' *(Ritch Shydner)*

My last husband charged calls to his girlfriend in Bolivia on my phone. I refused to pay and had to change the number I've had for 18 years. What I really missed after he left was the phone number. *(Viveca Lindfors)*

I met my wife at the travel bureau. She was looking for a vacation and I was the last resort. *(Tommy Cooper)*

Aristotle maintained that women have fewer teeth than men. Although he was twice married, it never occurred to him to verify this statement by examining his wives' mouths. *(Bertrand Russell)*

Men who don't understand women fall into two categories: bachelors and husbands. *(Jacques Languirand)*

My wife told me she bought a dress everytime she was down in the dumps. I replied, 'So that's where you get them.' *(Jack Cruise)*

American women expect to find in their husbands a perfection that English women only hope to find in their butlers. *(Somerset Maugham)*

'Did you hear Bridget is getting married?'
'Married? I didn't even know she was pregnant!'
  (Kevin Murtie)

In some marriages, one and one equals one. *(Calista Flockhart)*

My wife's father told me that if I married his daughter he'd give
  me three acres and a cow. I'm still waiting for the three acres.
  (Max Miller)

I'm still friends with all my ex's, apart from my husbands. *(Cher)*

Gentleman requires first class accommodation, full board
  in quiet guesthouse in seaside resort, where he can
  put up with is wife for the first two weeks in August.
  (Ad quoted by Patrick Myler)

My husband and I are either going to buy a dog or have a child.
  We can't decide whether to ruin our carpet or our lives.
  (Rita Rudner)

A man doesn't buy his wife a fur coat to keep her warm but to
  keep her pleasant. *(Seymour Hicks)*

I married him for better or worse but not for lunch.
  (The Duchess of Windsor)

Behind every successful businessman stands a wife with nothing
  to wear. *(Hal Roach)*

The critical period in matrimony is breakfast-time. *(A.P. Herbert)*

My brother got a girl into trouble. He married her. *(Fred Metcalf)*

Gay marriage will never work. It's hard enough when you have even one man in a marriage. *(Graham Norton)*

Heterosexual marriage is wrong. If God meant men and women to be together He would have given them both penises. *(Jack McFarland)*

I haven't known any open marriages, though quite a few have been ajar. *(Zsa Zsa Gabor)*

I saw a couple kissing in the street the other day. Up until that point I thought they were married. *(Emo Philips)*

Some women pick men to marry; others pick them to pieces. *(Mae West)*

I've been married. Now I just rent. *(Frank Sinatra)*